THE WORD OF THE MAYA

by

Ruth Lee, Scribe

1663 LIBERTY DRIVE, SUITE 200
BLOOMINGTON, INDIANA 47403
(800) 839-8640
WWW.AUTHORHOUSE.COM

© 2004 Ruth Lee, Scribe
All Rights Reserved.

No part of this book may be reproduced, stored in a retrieval system, or transmitted by any means without the written permission of the author.

First published by AuthorHouse 09/27/04

ISBN: 1-4184-9614-6 (e)
ISBN: 1-4184-9613-8 (sc)

Printed in the United States of America
Bloomington, Indiana

This book is printed on acid-free paper.

This book is dedicated to the many students who have arrived in time to study with The Maya.

Other Books by Ruth Lee –

The Making of a Scribe
How to Achieve a Life You Can Write About

Can You Pray?
We Are All Here to Seek the Way

**Within the Veil:
An Adventure in Time**

It's About Time!
Work for a NEW You

Acknowledgements

Since this is no ordinary work of an author and staff who write and edit, then get it printed, we will possibly shock some readers by first giving heartfelt thanks to all who are here in this time and place who asked for this work to be done for them.

For this reason we salute all in Spirit and The Maya past and present who have reached beyond the usual waves of events today to teach what is needed to free the entire world from its decadent ways so everyone can fly and reach the sky. This does not mean that this message was published without help from others, rather puts all their efforts into perspective.

Ruth Lee trance scribed, or took the dictation in Spirit, typed it out and produced the manuscript, then asked a student to help her produce the best possible outcome by combining their two energies on line and over time to give the world a preview of what will be and can be done when you cooperate in order to learn how to rise higher over time or ascend.

Julie Powell is an artist who is really a writer, but not yet fully aware of it. Here she is able to fulfill that side of her life, while demonstrating her art and what she has discovered about The Mayan Timekeepers who are lost in time. Her art enhances the text, and she is responsible for actually getting this book published now. We thank her much.

The world now has to perspire and think about how this book can immediately help individuals live better today and will help all who aspire to rise in time. We sense it is easy work for some, but not that easy for the average person. For that reason, we salute all who read and study with The Maya now.

About the Art

The original oil painting for the cover, black and white drawings, and graphic images placed at the beginning and end of each chapter were created by Julie Powell.

The pyramid with eyes looking toward the sky represents the expansive and universal vision of the Maya who studied the movements of the stars and planets in the heavens as well as great universal cycles of time. The rising sun visible in the top of the pyramid represents the dawning of higher consciousness and a beacon for those ready to contribute their own light to this world before returning to the divine source from which we have all originated.

The Timekeeper is adapted from Mayan images symbolizing the burden of time carried by the universe in order to allow our uniquely human perspective of time and space while we evolve on this plane.

The Scribe represents both the author, Ruth Lee who has channeled this book and many other books of wisdom as well as all scribes who serve humanity by bringing universal and spiritual lessons to earth from Teachers beyond our earthly plane.

The chapter head and end symbols both incorporate a hand, the physical means by which a scribe is able to bring wisdom to written form and make it available to those who would use it. The hand is also the basis of the Mayan calendar day sign Manik, Mayan birth sign of Ruth Lee. The chapter heads each contain a hand with a Mayan numeral corresponding to the number of each chapter. The chapter end glyph is a hand incorporated with a spiral and a highly stylized shell based upon the Mayan glyph for Zero.

The spiral is seen widely throughout Mayan art and architecture as a symbol of the Absolute, Origin of All, or God of All. It implies movement of energy in cyclical patterns emerging from a single source as well as a path back to the center of being. A spiral in combination with a shell is used by the Maya to represent not only Zero, but also the concept of completion, hence the use of this glyph at the end of each chapter.

I thank Ruth Lee and the Maya for the privilege of participating in this work. I also wish to thank R. L. Geyer of Aesthetic Endeavors in Asheville, NC for his cover title design, selection of cover fonts and invaluable technical assistance.

Julie Powell
June 26, 2004
8 Muluc, 16 Kayab

Introduction

The world is not round nor is it going to stop rotating now, but there are some things you must know in order to leave it easily and never come back or have to redo work you have put together ever so carefully over time. We, The Maya, speak of what is going to happen in ways that only a few will be able to discover within these pages immediately, others must study longer. We speak in waves over many pages to all who wish to seek a better way of life now and over time.

Today, look at what you are and what you came to Earth to be. Do you agree with the things you were taught when young? If not, what have you done to increase your abilities and your life so far? Are you wise and able to answer all of our questions without wondering why we ask them and who has the answers? You will go far if you answer, "I have to wait and see." You cannot agree with what you have not read or been taught, so hold onto whatever you believe now--then read and decide if you need to update your own work inside.

When a book of this greatness comes to be, there are many who cannot agree on who is allowed to receive it. We opened to the universe and found only one scribe alive in your world who could take down the content of our work. That one scribe was willing to take the time from her own life to give to The Maya so you could read it more easily. Are you worthy of this sacrifice? Decide and then move ahead and work diligently to ascend at the end. You will meet many then who are scribes and artists plus those who work to perform this miracle for you over time, too. Today, however, you can only see the final manuscript created through Ruth Lee, The Scribe, and our helper in this production, Julie Powell, who adorned the work with art and financed it.

This is not a storybook or a book about what you should think, but it is philosophy. You can adopt it or not, but it will change the way you feel about people who are not divine and people who are wasting your time. Be aware of that as you collect your talents. Have a wonderful year as you work hard to clear away whatever you had to do to get to the point where you are reading this line.

Table of Contents

Acknowledgements ix

About the Art xi

Introduction xiii

Chapter One
THE WORD OF THE MAYA 1

Chapter Two
MAYA WITHIN THE VEIL: THE THEORY OF TIME 13

Chapter Three
WHEN YOU ARE YOU 23

Chapter Four
JUSTICE, WORTH, WILL 35

Chapter Five
MAYA MOVE YOU WILL, TOO 49

Chapter Six
THE MISSION OF THE MAYA: HOPE 61

Chapter Seven
MAYA MAGIC 75

Chapter Eight
MAYA MEDITATIONS BEGIN AND END THE DAY 87

Chapter Nine
MIDDLE LIFE WAYS 91

Chapter Ten
MAYA BIRTH 107

Chapter Eleven
THE MAYA WORK FOR YOU 121

Chapter Twelve
MAYA WORK WITHIN THE VEIL 127

Chapter Thirteen
MAYA WORK WITHIN YOUR WORK 139

Chapter Fourteen
MAYA WRITING WITH WHAT YOU HAVE IN MIND .. 145

Chapter Fifteen
MAYA WORK - FOOD FOR YOU 161

Chapter Sixteen
MAYA MYSTERIES WITHIN THE VEIL 179

End Notes 191

Chapter One

THE WORD OF THE MAYA

We are The Maya!
If you are Maya, raise high the cup of the Lord!

We can boldly move into this world and assert our control, but we do not. We instead seek the bold. We seek the old. We seek the new way of being, living, and believing that is in the New Age, but we are here to see what you believe and why you survive when the old ways are not followed today.

What do you see in this work? Are you able to go berserk and believe that the devil of another religious faith would help you erase what you believe? You have no faith then, but you will end the old work now and begin to believe in You again.

We are not the same as you. We are not different from the essential being that is You; therefore, we want to work in the spiritual realm with you again.

Yes, we worked together long ago—and now you know. You have not picked up this book and begun to write and dream and sing as it asks had you not felt that you did it before with us. You would not have read this far. You would have dropped the book and looked at another or passed into another class, because this is the part of the book that makes you feel that you can last.

When you dream of the work you do, you have to follow that work through or you will end it then. What do you do now?

Are you able to stop and look and think of you? Are you? How many questions does it take to make you stop and look inside your mind? When questioned by a teacher or a leader, are you able to fully see that they believe in you? You do? Good for you!

When you are questioned and asked to look deep within you, please believe and do it for You. If you do not, the work stops.

If you stopped and cannot move now, you are still working on the book that preceded this one. We would ask that you stop and pursue the workbook and do what is asked, then return to doing this work for You.

We are commissioned by the Higher Force to work with you, but does that mean you are alone and off the 'beam'? No, but you are. You are not in the same time line as we are. You can change, but you probably think it would be a mistake to lose your place in this arcade of love and life where you are. We believe you can enter one time frame after the other. But why not stay as you are and dream to a deeper level than you can see and live there with us and be as is? We are.

The Word of The Maya

The third message you meet in any dream is what you are to do when you *awaken*. The second message is: What does it mean? And the first command is to remember what you dreamt. If you cannot at first recount all the symbols, then ask for help in discovering what the entire dream means because you will not be able to enter the beam again and move further from Earth once you are awake.

You are a dream! Think of how many times in this life you have exercised the will to dream and excused your mind by saying you could not remember a line? You were lazy and indifferent to time then, because it was there. You are also lazy and indifferent if you do not care about time but judge others by how prepared they are by this experience.

Are you rich and famous today? Are you unique in some way? Why are others here to speak with you then, and walk and talk with you again? Are you amazed, too? If you can say 'yes' to more than one question we asked now, you are on your way. Do most people recognize that you pray and that you know how to play? If not, you are not doing something for You that you alone know how to do at home now.

If you are not able to live as you and You and YOU, who are you? What do you want to do? Are you fully in love with the being who will love you--You? You will find that whatever love you have comes from inside the line that travels up the spine, and if the spine is interrupted at any time, you begin to see in others things other than love. You will now notice that one with a crippled or maimed spine is not as likely to love others even though they have a brain that produces emotions you often confuse with love. What do you think of others? Are you crippling or maiming you?

Ruth Lee, Scribe

What do you do?

Look at that line one more time.

What do you do to be you? Are you confused by simple questions about you? You then have to confuse the mind more to get into line and enter the mind at a time when you can cleanse it of what you are doing to you to make it confused about you. Such a sentence is designed to make the mind try to answer all the questions at one time in order to unkink the spine, but sometimes it does not work for you.

What to do if the mind controls you? You will work within you to relax and admit that you are prone to anxiety or depression and act. If you act, the anxiety and depressed emotions flow away and out from you into the work you do. If you sit, you are admitting you are too lazy to do it and prefer to be as is. We do not admit such lazy people into The Maya, but you will fit in if you remove the fit of temper within you and just do it.

You do what you do because you are who? Why do *you* hamper you? Are *you* who tries to make you feel that your mind is so real that nothing in spirit can enter it?

What did you do just now?

Enter the mind now and cleanse it. If you can do it, do it. If you cannot, sit still.

What did you do?

ARE YOU FIT TO BE A MAYA BEFORE THE END OF TIME COMES TO YOU?

Begin work within by repeating over and over again the following and watch what it does to you:

I am Maya. I live in the world. I exist now.

This is an affirmation of who you are that flows from You and will admit no one else ever into you, but you can still stop you from flowing and growing. You do that. You admit nothing. If you seek to be nothing within, you end the flow. If you do that, where will you go if you dammed up all emotion within you? Are we too slow for you? Are you ready to go?

If you die reading this book, try to admit that you have had the time of your life in order to flow and grow and develop within into the best spiritual being you have ever been. If you cannot do it, go. If you are able to promote the work you do within you, you will ascend and never limit the being you love--You. You will also have no time to go back and redo whatever you did not do--so go and do the work you know needs more work done in time for you to go.

Whatever you said just now to you worked or it did not. What? You either believe or you do not. It is not convoluted sentences that make you want to believe in you and the work of You, it is you. Your own belief system is what you grew. If you were preached to by people who intended to teach you, you watched everything they did to make sure they meant what they said to you. Do you now do that to you, too? You do.

If you talk about being a big person yet you are not, you diminish you into a shoe-string seam of energy or dream that is not big enough for you to explore all the areas you came to Earth to live and work on before you go to the next experiment. What made you admit that you were all air and not going to work within? You. You said it, then decided to make it never a reality. If you work at it, you do it. But if you sit and talk about you, what need is there for you to do it for You?

You do. You need to do. You feel that whatever you do is real and whatever is air is not there. If you talk, is that not air and not really there?

What did you do to make you feel good about you? What do you think others compare when they look at you and see you stare at them and not do what you say you will do? Are you there?

What you feel and the energy you reveal is not the same as it was? Your energy level is at a plus all the time you work and love, but discharges first from the work, then the love goes into reverse until all the energy is discharged and you feel depressed again by you. What to do? Ignore the fear within you and work. Do what you love? Why not? You get to choose what to do. If you prefer to martyr you, do it. But no one else wants you to do that--just you.

If your own work is not good, what do you think of others? You think that they do not work as you do. You think they are full of designs to drink wine and not work, if you do. You believe that some cheat and scam others because that is what you believe is smart to do. You think that others want money because you do. You gamble your life's work in order to sport a watch or a car or whatever, but who else wants one but you? No one. You are who decides what others want from you.

If you cannot imagine that you are loved just because you are, what do you think of others who are like you, too?

The Word of The Maya

If your mind cannot comprehend time, what is there that blocks you? Time is the mission of this lifeline and if you ignore that task, you come back to Earth to learn more and do more with it than you now do.

If your life is short and its mission was to do a little bit and then leave, would God grant you that feat? Why not? You are who designs this road, so make a fork in it and do what you love or do what you hate, but work to promote the end of this road and get on with it.

Your mind is not the same as The Maya mind, but it is. You have to live as a Maya inside to be able to blend at the tide of time when it arrives, but you do not have to live it. You can decide to renew the work in spirit. You can sit and ignore that time is rapidly explored by others who are better equipped to live than you are, but you do not like to admit it because you want to be better than all others on Earth. Admit it.

If you admit that you are shortsighted, and even-disposition enough to believe that this is love and that you have it all, you might decide to never move again within your own life, but God is on the other side waiting in the line of life to give it again. You will end this life regardless of how you live it now.

When you are free to believe in another, you have achieved a high level of belief in what you are and will be. But many achieve nothing and seem to believe in many who are not able to achieve. Why? You are who you are and will be until you decide to achieve or change the way you are. If you do not change and develop any other lane or path, you will have no divided highway leading to the new road in the next life. You will be exactly as you are at this time--and undecided about the new life.

Ruth Lee, Scribe

Your life is new every day or two
Do you see it now?

When you arrive at the end of one life, will you automatically be granted the opportunity to proceed? You better believe that life is not so permanent that you lose all time and perspective from one experience to another. You know inside that God is working all the time to abide within you and help you swim the tide, but you personally may not believe, and wish to do it alone. You will be allowed to do that, but do not blame God when the sea comes and overwhelms thee.

You will mind that we use the word 'thee' from time to time and may wonder about it, but we use 'you' in many cases to decide what you can be. The Maya are alive in the modern world, as is The Scribe, but you are not able to scribe the Maya as they are because the Scribes of The Maya are still in the next world. If you can see the Scribe who writes within Ruth Lee, you are able to believe. But if you cannot, see that The Scribe is an ordinary person writing to you about the world of The Maya and will discuss with you whatever you like, but will only read what The Maya scribe.

You will find that most people are not generous with time and will not obey the force of energy in their own line long enough to meditate to a deep enough level to work for The Maya as The Scribe does, but you may be able to deliberate for hours at a time with one of the tribe.

We congratulate you if you already do, but most will only grow into that work as we work in this world. You will find Maya in the world, but most do not know you. Why? You do not travel to them, but go abroad seeking others more and more like you--time and time again. The aboriginal peoples thrive in all parts of the world, but are the cultivated ones cultured enough to be able to appreciate them and what they have done? Are you cultured enough to visit the Maya and not look at them as if they live in a zoo?

You will find the Maya of this world are not petrified and scared of you, but you may be afraid that they will be holier than you. Do not do that to you. You are who is guided into that world and admitted into the tribe or not, but you are not expected to don the warrior's paint or the diviner's robe in order to fit into their place. You are who you are. Remain in your own line, but admit them to the point where you can divine within you what you wish to paint and do it for you.

If you can paint a mandala like Ruth, and do it so well that she is unable to decide if she did it for you, then you are Maya. You may not realize that she has met many Maya who are only now able to admit that they are alive to the art, too, but she does the drawings like no one else does. Why? You are not willing to let the artist within flow and do the work you know. She is.

When you flow and grow and decide what you are here to do and know, will you do it? Why do you not decide to do it now? Why? The ego alone is trying to postpone the advent of the calendar into your life. You have to do it alone. But since the ego knows nothing of it and despises whatever is not known, it refuses to let you abide in time.

If you can meditate within you for an hour a day and have no problems living that way, you will not have as many friends as you had, but will find more honesty in the ones who live with you and go places with you now. You will also not forget that those who live with you are those who admit that they want to be near you now. If you do not like it, you can ask them to move or go within and admit no one into you

Ruth Lee, Scribe

again. You can live as a monk in a tenement village, but not as a mayor of the Maya.

Your tribe is not the way you are?
You are Maya!

You have to be, to score such a high degree of adversity and live to talk about it never. If you talk always about the past and how much you had, you are not going to have much now. If you talk about the past as if another was there, you share too much. Beware! But if you share and work in the air, all is revealed to you and those who work with you. Do it –share there!

When your mind is full of the work of others, and you feel that you do not do as much, you envy them and constrict the work you do with them. Beware! If you hate anyone, you contain the poison within you. Beware! If you are unable to do much and think that another should be a slave to you, you will be asked to do much and not be paid. Why? Are you unable to decipher what you do? Are you who decides today what you will be? You are.

Think of the day. Think of you in an entirely different way. Now pray.

If you cannot believe in prayer and work on you that way today, you will not be able to end your day in the way we plan to ascend one day. You can prepare to do whatever you wish to do, but to ascend is the dream of The Maya, and we all prepare to end at the time when the calendar falls in line, but you can be whoever you are. We want to be free!

Scribed by Ruth Lee
August 1, 1997 - Portal day

Revised, May 4, 2004
Portal Day, Solar Eclipse, Full Moon

Chapter Two

MAYA WITHIN THE VEIL: THE THEORY OF TIME

What if your life exists as is always? What if you have no time to be anyone but this life? What if you could exist in several different lives at one time? Would this life be the one that sticks or would there be another that comes before this--at the same time as this--or after this? What makes you feel this is it?

When you decide to live, you exist. But if you sit and do very little at this time, it may be that you exist in another state of mind and that state of mind is just a matter of time. What do you decide when you decide to reside always in one lifetime? You decide to provide the message and tools that will make that one life sublime, or you decide it is not the time for you to totally commit to being you as if it were the only time.

Once you decide to commit to a life, you do it! But if you are uncommitted to doing anything now, does that mean you are unable to commit and are not living as if you had a life? It does.

When your life is full of activities and gifts and others speak of you with love, you are totally committed to it but could slip into another avenue or two before that life is through and not do much at all for you. What is then done to you? You decide to move. You decide to commit to another or you try to live in another side of you.

We know many in insane asylums are there because of the need to be somewhere where they are seen in a different light and can exist as is, but what did you decide happened to them in this life? You never bothered to even try to figure out what could or does change in a person's mind? You are lazy at best and foolish at worst if you decide to not fully explore the mind in this time. It is there to help you and be used as a tool, but only fools will use what they have and not see that it cannot last.

If you are a fool, are you going to admit that you believe that the mind controls time? Are you going to say to you at this time, I know all about time? Are you ready to ignore what others compare and store in their computers about you and the things you do? What do you think of others?

'What' is a powerful word, but not if you ignore its meaning. If you ignore the powerful, and the powerful get nervous around you, you will perish in a moment. Remember that.

What did you get from all of that paragraph and what it consists of at this moment?

You are not prepared to be you?
Who is?

The Word of The Maya

Are you ready to move up into the next year or two? Why always ask what the future will bring when you do not live today? It is a fool's way to get away from working hard. Since all see that it does work on some days, many will try to perform feats of magic in a way to get you into the next day. Are you doing that, too?

Are you able to skip ahead and live in the next day? You may, but you seldom remember it. Most dreams skip around from time to time and seldom seem to display the seam that keeps them all tucked in and not fray into today, but some of you do stay there. Some of you decide to continue a dream day after day and not display a thing about the dream to others who are on Earth today. What would you be if you lived like such a person today? You would be listless and restless and depressed in a serious way.

What if you go from city to city trying to find rest and it does not exist in any city you visit, but perhaps the one you missed? That is a game people play with others all day. You run from one person to another at parties hoping the next one is going to be the one who is there to soar and take you away with them, but you are who you were when you opened the door and not likely to move away or change.

We are The Maya. We move into the time line and exist within a time and then soar to another plateau and do more-- but what do you think of the time?

What do you do about the time?

When you are bored and tired of being as is, what gives you the desire to do more?

What is the time?

Ruth Lee, Scribe

Look at those three lines again.

Look once more.

The line you are doing over and over again in your mind is reminding you to begin again. If you do the same work over and over and over and over, you will find in time a beginning--start over there. Knitting a sweater is one way to find how your life is put together, but painting is a better way if you have little time left to you today. Why? You get to create and complete the work in a single day.

Your mind is always on time, but you may not believe it yet. We do, but you may not see that the veil of electricity within you is not as great as you when you are into the veil, too. You are a body, and a mind, and a spirit? You are more than these when combined, but three is a powerful number that splits unhappily in time. You will side with the mind if your body is out of order for a time and try to make the body pay for whatever you are spiritually disinclined to see that day, or you will attack the spirit with the body and mind in a dynamic duo inclined to pine over men or women all the time. You do not do that?

'Good' is when you are able to stand by anyone who is good and kind. But is it 'bad' to turn your back on the evil inside others at any time?

What makes you shirk hard work?

When the mind becomes cluttered with matters that are of little or no use to you, you can corrupt your thoughts and begin to discuss others as if they were not clever, were not as good as you, or were evil because they are not like you. Think not of the importance of you and what you do, but of what such evil and demonic thoughts could do to you. You corrupt your mind if you do evil to others and then call them demons and such because they do not believe as you do. You will be chastised if you do that, and they will most likely turn around and do it back to you.

Why karma?

You believe in it, so it works to control the work of the world. If you believe the world is great and going to help you go places, you aspire to work hard and do whatever is required. If you believe that no one is going to love you, you will not achieve and you will disbelieve that others admire you or what you do. You die young and do nothing that you would have done if loved by your mother. That is the truth, but some of you will not deduce the power of youth.

You are a youth? You are young only if you cannot find one who is younger than you. Once you find another younger than you, you become older than the other and have to stand up for the young, so you are no longer the youngest one in the group and have to move up. If you refuse to grow and assume more and more responsibilities than you have to, you will be stunted from that time forward, but it does not make you young.

You are who you are. If you assume that age is a difficult subject and one you will always avoid, you are stunted by the idea that you have not yet begun to live. If you are at that stage, begin at once!

If your mind is inside the trail of tears that amass at stages from the past, live it out and see what makes you pout. Do not live in a veil of water when you are electrically charged. Do not live in a time that is not going to give? You have to live, so get going with it.

If your mind expects others to give to you all their time, you are stunted from the time you became such a beggar. But if you exist merely to give, you give up all that you should be amassing now. Why amass energy and gifts? You will live a better life if you can exist and give as much you want. If you give everyone a gift each day or stay away from others for many days, what happens when you show up to meet the clan? You are greeted with a loud "Good Day!" Otherwise, you are not noticed unless you continue to give gifts or stay away.

You are who is going to reside within you or the 'veil,' as we say. You are who goes each day to work in the world or not, but you always stay inside you and work on you all day--regardless of what you might say.

When your mind is a thin sheet of pine, are you able to sit there and watch the roots intertwine over you from time to time? No, but you could. You could become the pine and live in a way that is nourished from the body of today. It happens and can become a way to establish the work you will be one day; but seldom do you even see a tree as possibly being thee. We see, but you refuse to accept that view, too. Why?

You might delight your mind at times by assuming an animal is like a human in many ways. Humans are unkind for no reason and animals stay away when they are aware the enemy is near. What about those reactions seems similar? Neither, yet you will deceive you into believing a dog or cat or rodent will be an acceptable substitute for an adult human being. What happened to you when you were young? Look back and realize what you are doing now. If you still like the animal and it provides you with fun or something to do, then that is all right, but never substitute a cat or dog for another who is not able to sit and wait for you to decide what to do.

Look at the thin tissue that makes up the body of you. Is it the same as it was when you were 22? You are younger than that? Good for you, but assume you are going to move and live to be more than age 22. What will you do when you are older than you are today and able to say, "I was once as young as you?" What will that make you?

When the old are tired and unable to stay any longer, they pray. Do you?

When you get old and tired and unable to pray, will you stay?

What if you were old and tired and stayed and had no time to pray?

What in those three lines sings today? Look inside you and pray. Whatever you feel is real. If you cannot sing within or outside the body again, you might as well not be alive. Why? You cannot enjoy this life anyway, so why not soar away?

The Maya!

What about that phrase makes you sing inside you today? You will find that The Maya are here within you and able to sing and dance and commit to being on time within you, but not if you are unable to admit you are Maya. If you admit you are a Maya, will it commit some unpardonable sin within you today? What about tomorrow?

Your mind is not able to sit and do nothing whatsoever, so it commits unpardonable sins and does nothing within all day. You are made to work on your own life, but is it the life you admit? What of it? You are then not doing what you want with it.

If you live and die a Maya in your mind, what do you think others will see when you pass before them in a flow? You will go in a flash and never flow as a Maya. You flow as you grow, but when you pass, you go in a flash--if you are Maya.

What makes a Maya?
You know!

You have within you a line of prosperity and a line of power that makes you want to use it all the time, but most humans are too slow in your own time this time to know. You let others talk you into work that will never give you enough of what you want to know. That slows you down and keeps you in the same power until you go.

What do you know?

That is the power of your soul. The power? The power to move and to grow. You are who you are! You are Maya always in these times, and if you want to know who they are, go to the mass of energy you stored away in the last days of The Maya who came before.

Your mind cannot absorb more. We are able to see that today you have found a way to open wider, but to open too fast is to pry the spring into a leap that it cannot complete, yet still spring back, so we go and let you repeat this lesson in time over and over until you feel it is the time to do more.

Chapter Three

WHEN YOU ARE YOU

Whatever you do and wherever you go, there are people who are going to know you and want you and desire you, but do you? Are you able to love you? If you never do, you ignore the God of All restored and abiding within you. What can you do? Understand what is you and what is God. You do know, but you might not think of it now.

Your mind is a place. Your body is a means of transporting you all over this place, but you are the being. You are who exceeds or *bes* or does not do anything you please.

Remember to always see and look at you and what you do before you look at another and try to do what they do. If you do that first, you begin to envy and feel jealous of those who are not going to want to know you. Who loves those who envy or are jealous of them? No one.

You have found that many enemies abound? You know them? You are permitting your own view of you to permanently spot the envy and jealousy abiding within you and in others, too. You are able to see the hate if that is what is spiting you. If you could just see the love inside you, what do you think others would see in you, too? Love.

Do you want to love? Do you want to sit and let others do it for you? Are you so lazy in spirit that you cannot permit you to sit and adore the world and the work of God? You are? Then at least you can admit that you need to work on you.

We begin with you. If you do not admit a thing about you, how can you open or enter into the world that is you and change anything that is amiss? You do not. God could but will probably let you learn the hard lessons of this life again rather than let you do anything unkind or evil to others who are trying to move upward and out of this bend in the line once again.

You are all in a line. You all sit at times and blend within that line, but most of you work all the time and try to align your appointment books to time while sitting on the tip of your spine and do not understand what time is about this time. Why? You think you know it all. You do, if you never see you or talk to God at all.

What if?

Who cares about you?
What do others think of me and you and others?
Who cares?
You!

You is the smaller version of You, and You is a smaller version of YOU, but God of All controls the total being of All.

The Word of The Maya

You are small, and you have to know why you are allowed to live at all? You are small and allowed to do what God has prepared for you to do; however, most sit and watch others achieve, then try to run them over. Does that describe you? Are you trying to unscrew the bulb that lights the world? Are you trying to diminish the light? Are you easily frightened by others talking about God? If you are, you are very, very, very small. But if you can accept that others might not like you or care about you, you can rise taller and be wider than ever.

Why would you weed out the life of another? You are the planter of seeds, but many of you plant too many seeds to ever be able to know what you breed. Why? You want to have sex, and you see it as fun, but it is not funny when you proceed to have an unwanted child. Why do you find fun in sex anyhow? You are not able to imagine anyone wanting you as you are now.

Think of everything you talk about to others

What did you think about? Are you able to spout off endless stories about what you do and why you are successful, too? Are you able to talk for almost an hour about something funny that happened to you? Why not? Are you expecting everyone else to entertain you for an hour or more and unwilling to do it, too? You are a bore if you are.

You are who dedicates this life to love or whatever, but you might as well get over wanting others to love you. Why? They must always stop and do that first for themselves or they will not be able to love you. You do that? You love so many others that they can feel it radiating from you? Good for you and good for all who are blessed to work and live around you! What if we called them all and asked them what you do? Would you be willing to give them as a reference or talk about you?

If your idea of being loved is to be noticed or fondled or even caressed, you have to have a lot of sex to make up for love that comes from the heart. But you and your mind will not part if one person after another drops you from the list of promising partners in order to love someone else from the heart. The heart attack of losing someone who truly loves you is what hurts you now? You then loved. If you are not afraid to pick up partners among the crowd around you, you do not love at all. You are merely seeking someone to drop you when their time comes to do whatever they truly want to do, too.

You could line up a lifetime of people who will drop you, or you could find one or two partners who truly remind you of you. What do you intend to do? You already did it for you? Great! We want you.

If you can entertain and keep a partner for many years doing the same thing always, you must have more than those who cannot score or do not have the stamina to stay in one relationship for many years and do the work and the tears to end all their own fears. If you fear too many people, you are who will rescue you. If you have no fear, God will take the fear out of being near and follow you from place to place in order to make sure you arrive at each destination.

Use Fear!
Notice what is not wise to do...

Notice that fear is inside you because you are not safe or you are about to do something unwise. Have you not noticed that happening to you?

If you do not notice you or others, you must fully expose you to the truth because you are a fool. You have to accept that as a condition of being in this state of ambition where you do not care about you or others. You have to erase many things you do at this time and place, but whatever you do, do not let it all come unglued at once.

If you are here, God performed it for you and asked that you be allowed to enter into the present framework of this country or society--to be as you are. If you cannot accept that, you will feel very bad and unable to exile you. But if you love you and enjoy the space you occupy today and expect to do more and more before you fly, you are in the right time.

You *and* your mind have time, but the body has only a season or two to be, then it is gone for all time. It is not reused. You do not resurrect the body in one space or expect it to come back as is in another space. If you do, erase that lie from within your mind. You will return!

You will realign within to others who lived within your time, but not as a body. You represent the body of Christ, but you are not the body realized at this time. You are all in this time to realize that you have bodies and spines that can be overdoing many things that in simpler times would have helped you, and this is the time to realign within you and use the spine to begin to channel that which is outside of you.

You have channeled?

You know then that no one can enter you or take you over, but you can pick up the means to communicate with those who are also working to be in this time continuum with you. You do that? Good. We need teachers to help The Maya to be as worthy of the task as when God asked, but if you are not able to teach, please erase your own mind's mistakes. Why erase mistakes? You need to be open to the correct attitude.

If your mind is misaligned and you are unhappy today, you have not stayed long enough in a state of grace and unable to amaze you today. Stay in grace and sit there for the hour or two that it takes you to be sure you are of God. You will score a ten in every game you pursue or do what you adore then. You do not have to play games if you have work that needs to be done, but if you prefer to have fun, play games until the next day has begun. Why? You are not done.

You will find that games are easy to explain, but life is not if you only want to have fun. Life is too complex and the issue is too hard for you to readily communicate unless you know how to channel within you to others near you or willing to listen to you. We would love to listen to you. Why not channel now?

When you desire something esoteric, or convoluted by nature, do you expect someone else to do your work to get through it? You do? Then you will fail this class and not be able to see who is going to leave you for all time if you do that. You will also have to leave, but this Earth is not going to last long enough for you to do such a life over and over.

When a world is over and done with, What happens to it?

You move to the next experience--and many of you are ready for it. You want others to end their game, too, but many of you do not care if they ever do. What to do? Get over it! Go inside you and see why you are willing to ascend and not take anyone with you again.

If your mind is so extended that you could bend a spoon with it, why would you? You need to use the power you conceal within you to better you. If you have done all you came to do, extend you into the next work of You. See? You can find out about You, but first you have to do all you came to do.

You are who is the very essence of You, but if you appear not to be able to scout out company in the next view, you might be alone for quite a few moons. If you go inside you and find no companion at home, are you the one who is lonely? You are? Surely you are able to make friends and sit at a table, but does that excuse you from doing the work you came to do? Never, but there may be within that group a friend who is there to help you or you need to help to move ahead, too. You have to wonder why you would be there and not with others, too. Do you?

When you go for an outing that seems to be too much of a chore to you, are you trying to say you are bored? You are. If a chore is not very boring to you, you will be interested in it to the degree that it can fatigue you and make you believe in those who are there with you and able to explore them. If you have no degree of accomplishment that you can perceive, you will not like to explore or work with others. Explore more.

When you begin to spy upon what others do, you have to work on the inner you most of the time. If you watch them, you are not doing what you know you could do, and you want them to explore for you. Why? You are a moral coward and want them to end whatever they doing then.

You will find that the coward is not the one who takes uncertain risks time and time again, but the one who works at being steady and profound and does whatever he or she wishes. You are a coward if you cannot invite people into your home and enjoy them because you fear others. You are a coward if you think others would be upset if you were to act like yourself--so you do not. What kind of moral issue do you have to complete before you are fearless? That one that keeps you from having fun all day long and meeting others.

Moral cowards abound

There are so many in some towns that they do nothing but what is currently in fashion and never talk about another who is doing whatever they want. Do you live in such a way today? Why not be fearless and send that town a message? Try to live your own way. You are afraid? What do you say about people who do live with God and pray? Look at you. Are you doing the same?

What kind of life do you now refuse to accept as being the right way to live today? Are you afraid of the sexually unrestrained or what they might say if you do not act like them today? Are you afraid of those who have more expenses and less money than you or those who are living in the reverse from you? What do you say?

Are you afraid? Remember, we are aware of the fate of those who do not hesitate to lie to themselves and never do what they came to do, but are you?

When you find the time to dance and sing and have fun, do you? Are you aware of the time? Are you afraid of the work you have to do to gain the power of being you? Are you afraid of You?

When you decided to study the Mayan Calendar, did *you* decide or did You? Are you aware that many of you just glide into and about and bump into things rather than plan to live this life as it was meant for you to do? Are you one who laughs when something is not clear to you? We truly despise the 'comic' who hates you and tries to do you in, but do you?

Work on the life within you. Work on the world that exists beyond you. But do not mix the issue of the one or the other until you know what to do. You have to win. You have come to this world to do what you already know how to do. Work on fully completing you and doing your work, then moving others to do what they came to do, too.

You are here to raise children?

You may decide that you know the way and you want children to continue to work with you, but almost no one today really wants to raise kids. If you do, please handle this life with a feeling that bliss is waiting there when you are through. You will be released from all necessity to complete work for them once they are adult at 18 or 22, or when you are able to let them swim alone, but do not worry about having them by your side at the end of this life. You will be alone.

You came into the world alone--except for you, and God within You, and a guide or two to help make sure you make the next shore on time, but you will go out with the same tribe. You are not here to die alone? You are here to live as you, and be you, and thrive. If you have to do it alone, then be wise enough to see that it is how you wish to be. Enjoy this life. If you wish to have company, take the price tags away and enjoy the ride, if that is what you believe it is to be. If you do not, then enjoy the added responsibility. You achieve more if you do add responsibilities to your life.

You will find that most people sit too much to enjoy what they do in this life, but being employed is not a joy. You are in joy? Good. You would achieve regardless of what you might do to be employed. If you are angry at others who work beside you and refuse to forget them when the day is through for working with you, you are in trouble. You are upset with you. You are also upset that you do that to you.

Why?

Look always into your own eye. If you find a sty within your eye, you will not look fondly at anyone. You will not like the view of anyone around you. You will feel they are not good enough for you *or* any other way of seeing life today. But if you can enjoy looking at others through the veil that You provides you, you will always enjoy this life. We admire those who do that, but so few do that we wonder why all of you want to do it now.

We are all The Maya who came to Earth with you, but we are not here today in the human condition because we decided it was not our mission. You asked to be alive when the end of this time arrived, so the world is more crowded than it would have otherwise been. You all want the wars to stop and you all want to accomplish a lot, but the time is not going to stop. You are not able to get your own kind into the thread of time.

You will find that a tribe or two will escape without a trace, but most of you are too far off the beam to be able to erase all you are and will be in this time. You will have to do more. You will have to erase time and do it with grace.

When time is erased you do not care what others say to you? You are so in tune with others that they need not speak to you. You know by their face what they are and see inside any disgrace they hide, or you know by the air they breathe into their aura what they are thinking of becoming and what they are achieving. You know that now, but what do you do about achieving it for you?

You will find that today is a measure of time that you do not have to accept, but if you do, it means you are on time and will work harder than you would have if you had not regulated today and the way it moves within you. Do you follow that line? Then you are on time. If you could not understand it and wanted to end it, you are behind. If you could see the direction, but could not stop to unwind, you are too far ahead. You have to do all things in the same time.

If all of you read this book and all of you achieve the same look, will you all be able to meet and then ascend as a group? Why not try? You will try? Great! But before you commit anymore, be sure to follow to the end of the books and read those pages. You have to return to the Book, but not before you do the next chapter and more for you. We are not here to help you to ignore the work or to ignore others who are here and came before, but to demonstrate that you are not risking enough to be you if you cannot work on you without fearing what others might think of you.

Think more of YOU

Do what you adore and look at the door that opens wide within You.

Did you visualize the sky?
Did you open the door wide?

Ruth Lee, Scribe

You can and did visualize it easily if you ever before worked on the work of The Maya. If you did not do either and think it is a trick, you have to do more to find out what you fear and why. If you can accomplish that in one lesson or two, you will be admired, but The Maya are not here to admire you. The Maya are here to exist in this time and help all who risk and wish to ascend.

We want you with us, but it is your list of what you want to do—not ours. List all the times you ever were you, then list beside it what made you feel that way. Do it.

If you cannot commit to writing a list, you will not study time deeply enough to be involved in it. This lesson was all about you and your ability to assume that a higher You is in charge of the final view of this time. Why not do it all now?

Chapter Four

JUSTICE, WORTH, WILL

When you are alive and well and fully in charge of your own life, look at others then. Until you are, do not bother. Know that You are. You are the one who is in charge of you now.

Do you understand what is meant by the words 'you are'? Do you understand that as you are is the way you are and are to be dealt with now? If you have a problem with you now, change you into someone who will be different from whom you are now. Yes, you may use whom or what or some other word, but the sense is still the same, and you are who is going to remain exactly as you are--unless you change. If you try to change and cannot, you have found the strength of your will or will power. But if you remove all obstacles easily from you, your mind is stronger than you are.

Ruth Lee, Scribe

What did you do when you saw the word 'Justice' at the beginning of this chapter? Nothing? Why? Are you surprised that we wonder why?

You are born into a clan or a time or a grand design of life, but each time it is changed by a matter of time, and what that particular line wants to work on and develop and explore or ignore, but you are. You are now in a time when justice is the primary word. Did you realize that? Are you aware of your time? Do you understand the design?

What time do you feel inside?
What kind of line does it reveal?
Are you able to feel?

When you design a list of people, do you exist? What does that line or list of names mean to you? Are they there or just a figment of you? What does the mind do to remind you? Are they real? Do you just assume that they feel as you do? Why would you be able to feel as they do?

In the end of a line is a bit of residual of what was not done or used or was thrown away in a time of confusion, but in these times all is in fusion and you are all going to be used. You are going to find out why all are used. If you cannot, you will not ascend in the end as a complete line of friends.

If one of you is unable to fuse to anyone, what does that do to everyone?

Justice is defined in your own mind, but do you use what you find? Are you always doing what the mind refines and says is good for you to do? What do you feel will be the best view of you? Always think of the things you wish to do, why you feel that you could do it for you, and then do it.

The Word of The Maya

If you were to fuse into a brand new you, what do you think that person would do? We could work on you or destroy the work you do, but only you do you. Only you can destroy you or corrupt you or do what you have to do.

When the fuse is lit and you are all set, will you take off like a rocket ship?

What makes you feel like you?

When your mind is full of what you do and you compare it to others, does anyone else matter to you? If so, list them and figure out what they give to you or you take from them. If it is very much, you must get in touch and give it back and return it again with the interest and love that it deserves since you are not to take what you cannot produce or will not work to do. If you do, you will be reduced.

If you earn your bread and potatoes every day or so, you are never without food. But if you eat of what others have left over, you may one day be without food. Do you deserve it? We think those who work have no desire to feed you, so do the work, too. If you feel there is no justice in that, look at you. What do you do? Why should the universe take care of you?

Where is justice? What does it do?

Who takes care of You? YOU. If YOU is the last line of defense and the arbitrator between You and the God we all know to exist, what does YOU know about you and do for You?

Think! Are you still sitting and reading and not filtering anything through to You? We listen to all of you brag and boast about the work you do, but what do you know? If your mind is so big, what is it doing in such a small lifetime as this?

What if your mind exploded and you were let go? What would you know? Are you even capable of picking up after you go? Think and know, or sit and do nothing and feel what happens. It is going to happen, but most of you want to know when.

What to do when your mind refuses to tire or read or do what you know you must do in order to succeed? You read and reread until you hear it inside the lines being read to you one at a time. We watch a woman read and reread all the lines at one time and then go. She never really knows. She just goes to the next book and never slows. What is happening to her? She is lost in time.

You will know if your spurned love is not coming back to you, but will you want to admit it? You might see a psychic and ask for proof, but what if that person says only what you want to hear? You are filled with mirth and believe for all you are worth! But if the psychic or whomever you ask says it will not occur, you get mad at that person. When you do such an injustice once, you will fully experience it yourself. If you consistently do it, you become an inconsistent person and cannot be consoled regardless of what it is you are upset about within or want to rid your mind of now. You are who mixes the metaphors and makes your mind sore.

Remember to always listen. If you cannot, stop the process and block. If you block incoming messages until there is time to process what you already have inside, you will not be overset by new information. But if you constantly admit that you do not know whatever it is, you will in time become somewhat of an idiot and not be able to function in this time.

If the computer has you totally upset, you need to confront the problem more. Why are you upset? Why do you ignore that it acts the way the world prefers to move and does whatever it has to do? What makes you sure it will not work? You.

When you are sore and upset with another, look first to you and ignore what the other knows or does to you or whatever. Sit and look at you. Go inside and admit that you made the mistake that they now replicate. You see it, but you are tired of working on it. You want to move beyond, but they are dragging you into it. Once again, admit it. Sit. Do it if you must, and get beyond it.

If your mind is not going to be kind, desert it. That means you have to leave your own kind and never admit what you are in this time. It means you have to take up life in a strange land and wear different clothes and do whatever the natives permit. It means you cannot go back again or readmit yourself to the lessons they teach. If you cannot do it, stay as you are and work harder to know more about where you are and why you asked to be there.

If you switch the basics at all, you get outside the parameters of your existence and do not have time to work on the really far-out work you came to Earth to produce now. If you cannot accept that you are male or female again, what day do you suppose will arrive before you can begin the work you have come to do? Death will interfere more than you know by the time you go, but at least be ready for it. Do not fight the inevitable with all the breath you have in your store. Look at you more. Accept. Think more of what you are. Adore what you are and have and do and will proceed to be. Be.

When you change the body to make you more attractive, do you see that you change only your body and not the eye with which you see? You are who is not pleased. If you had a body covered with a rash or whatever, would you see it as a tattoo that God has given you? Would you be upset and never go about where others might see it and laugh? It is how you see and what you feel that determines the way you feel. Others might laugh, but you are who is upset by you--not by what they do.

You admit that God is mysterious, but what do you think of others who are more powerful than you? Look at the view of them now and see why you envy them or are jealous of what you refuse to do--be powerful, too.

What is power and why do you feel it? You are a power, too. You have power now, but you want others to come up and give you their power, too. Why not use what you have? Your sense of power will often permit you to overtake or undo a mistake, but will you?

Justice is the prevention of mistakes that take away the power of others. Do you feel that is the way to live within you? Are you afraid? What did you see that made you feel free?

When the power of God is loose in the world, what do you see? Lightning and electricity are power and ways that God is able to make known the path of your destiny. Are you using either to be? You see, you do not know what you have.

Your mind cannot see electricity, but you believe that someone else can wire you and change the fuses, too. What do you believe is going to happen if the power goes off inside you now? See what we mean? What explanation do you have?

If your mind is blank every time someone dies, you eat up a reserve you have put away. Why not sit and decide today what happens so that when you die it will not take so much time to figure out why. You will be able to quickly move to the other side.

If you hate to talk about death or dying or the ill or the aged, what is it that you fear inside? You. You alone feel scorned and alone or you are the one who believes you will be immortal and all others will age. Why try to stop the aging process? You do not see you as you are. You believe you are fooling others because you are a fool over you, but it seldom ever comes out that way--normally, you age. If you are genetically structured to age less and less as you grow older, you might be able to say you slowed your age by a day, but it never goes beyond the time established in the olden days.

You are who you are, and know, and work around all day. If you cannot associate with what you do and know and you feel funny if kids or oldsters are slow, you will slow down so much you will not be able to fully understand what you know. Why? Poetic justice is served. You have to experience everything once.

If you do deserve a lot of credit and nobody cares that much, what happens then? You get your just rewards, but maybe only at heaven's door. Once in a life you will be lauded and given a lot of presents, but it may not happen again. If it does, you earned those gifts. At least once you were given far more than you deserved. That is the way of justice.

Justice prevails. If you do not agree, then remind your mind to overstep the traces no more. If the mind cannot stay in line, why would you believe others' lives should stay in line? If you are upset and nervous, look at the refined and observe why they stay in line.

If your mind is still on time, you feel inside a sense of the world. Do not grieve if someone goes before his or her time. If you are not working and have no time, you will be upset every time someone goes before you think they have had time to fully work on the world.

Your mind is what you need to be? You know better, but still proceed to live as if the mind is where you dwell all the time. If the science of today makes you feel better in some way, use it more. If religious affiliation is what keeps you in touch, do that work and fully enjoy it today. If your mind loves to read and enjoys good books and stories that talk about you and what you do, enjoy them, but remember you are not living as they do.

If your mind is so full of books and tools and art and work that others produce, you might envy them. Why? You know you should contribute something, too. If you use what others produce, you have used up what you could now do. If you are able to reproduce their work, please do. Better yet, do a new work and make it something that only you can do. Perhaps they will envy you.

What you do and how you proceed
Depend upon your need

If your mind needs to do much, your body may not be able to keep up with you. If the body is unable to do all the things you want to do, rethink why you want them so much and cannot do them.

If you discover that you abuse the body in order to stay as young as you were, you have mindfully done an injustice to you. You will reap the rewards or lack of respect as you do anything else in this world. The body need not repent for getting old, but you do if you cannot accept it. When you grow old, what does it do to you? You are who you are and what you do, but do you see that or are you trying to act like you are young still?

What kind of friend are you? Are you able to respect the work of all who forget that they have friends when they get into their work? Are you able to forget their neglect? Are you sure you do not dislike the friends who admit that they at times would rather work than be with you? Do you respect your work, too?

What about work makes you feel that it gets to you? What do you do? Are you unable to complete projects and do anything all the way through? You will then have a lot of work to redo. You will find your life may be through and you still have too much to do. That is why we are here to remind you. You are to work out the problems of this life so you can rise and end this time, too.

When the world ends, you will fly? You have time to be you then, too. You have time to ignore what you do, too. But whatever you do, make sure you do not feel annoyed.

If you are enjoying a scene and a fly bothers you, why? What are you going to do today? Are you about to fly away? Are you going to sit and enjoy it? Will you meditate part of the day? Will you fully explore what you know now? Are you hiding and frowning upon others so they will not stay? Work and do what you enjoy and move beyond today.

What you do is not the same as it was, but it is you who stays. Work on that thought.

What does it mean? Were you able to understand and develop a new seam? A seam is a thought that is achieved and the dream realized, and you became that dream and are still alive. Seams show where you are and what you seem to be at this time, but they can rip and produce a rent about the time you end a life. Please repair all seams now open or unable to close.

You deserve this life

You will find others do not notice what you do well or very good, but will point out what you did not do. Why? They are there to guide you through the times when the mind decides you do not have to work or you have no time. You are told to do the work better or create another or it will not be sold to others. It is how you know you have to do it over.

Your mind is full of remorse? You produce the work of you, so go back and forth and redo whatever the work did to you and make sure the seam is whole and not going to break through to you. If you do, all things will then be good for you and you will move forward. The reverse might then be true, but justice is sometimes a long time in arriving. You decide. What do you do and when do you want to make sure you are all the way through this life? Decide.

What you do when you decide is make up your mind. You decide what to do and when to do it and how much to pursue and who is to know you, then you do it. If you do not decide, the work is strewn about and may not be delivered at all. It is your life, so decide what you want to do and who will help you, too. Work first on you.

The Word of The Maya

What you do when you decide to work on you is feel really good, at least at first. If you cannot, you are still upset with you. Once you do see why you are not able to do what you want to do or perhaps when you want to do it, you will find that you alone are the one blocking you and keeping you from flowing and growing. It is you doing it. No one else gives enough to know what you know. You alone control the destiny flow of you, so go within and take care of you again.

Every time you feel really low, go inward. Look at you and pray for the day when you will know the way. Ask for help and guidance and move in the way you are guiding you to go today, but move slowly. If you are not listening inside, you may decide to make a large purchase and blame others when it does not work. You may even say it is done in spite if another can buy and you cannot. Work hard. You are who is deciding how much debt you will hold--not others. You decide, so you must realize why.

If your mind is full of the past and its lost desires, you might traumatize the mind by saying you cannot last. The body will then die. The body listens inside. If you no longer want it, it will try to die as soon as it has time. You are who is then interfering with the process. You can heal your self if the soul is taught what to do in time.

Visualization will not help you if the body is diseased because it is time to go, but it will help those who triggered the need to go. Why? You programmed the mind and can rewind it. If you are already programmed at birth, you might delay the death by a day or so but not much beyond it. The body is not built to stand up to the advancement of time beyond the age when you came to Earth and asked to stay. If your work is not done, you have done that yourself. You are who is now on the line, so do more for you.

We want you to sit!
Can you obey?
Do it!

Did you sit? Good for you! Now admit that it was easier to just do it. Why? You have been told over and over in this book what to do, but you resist it. If you now just do it, you are now in charge of the mind and able to let God provide. If you cannot sit or obey or do it, you still think you provide all things for you in this time. Do it!

If you think your life is full of what you do for you, do it all then and never again pray to God for any help. You are in charge now. You will do it all. If you feel you want to do as much as you can, then let God do it, you are not in the right vein today but could slip into it tomorrow. If you are only on time half the time, you are still late. If you only believe in God when it is hard and there is no one else around to help you do whatever you want to do for you, then you do not believe at all. You either admit that you decided what this life was to you or you let it fall and damage you. Why did you live that way? You wanted to have it all.

If you do nothing at all, are you fit? Not if the body is not used or you are full of stuff you ate and never do anything with it. If you are full of whatever and do not feel good, are you a fool? You are full of it. You do not have to be so full of it, but it is you and what you do that makes you so much of a fool over it.

The Word of The Maya

What life is this? Who are you? **What did you do?** Who read all this to you? Are you going to remain full of all this, too? Are you going to use it?

Chapter Five

MAYA MOVE YOU WILL, TOO

Work is not the hardest of all things for you to do, but working before you have learned enough to change you spiritually enough to move forward is what hurts you. You do not intend to hurt you, but you do if you do not work within, too.

When you concentrate within and decide that you can begin, do you follow through and do it then? Are you willing to score the tests of this life and admit that once or twice you did not do the work and cheated a bit? If so, you are willing to admit to anything. You are not cheating You when you do nothing within, but you are denying you can go within and thus help you win.

The time is now only if you are concentrating upon it. If you do not like the present and what it continues to bring, you will turn into another avenue and follow it instead. But if you are now in the present and want it to go further than it is, you must begin to work within and ask what to do next.

Ruth Lee, Scribe

If your mind is unable to smile at you or do much for you, you are unable to control it. Before you begin to do anything more, go inside the mind and control the time. Reset the clock you use inside now. Tell you and you and you to align and get in time all the way down the line. If you do not, You will have nothing much to do and will sit idle. You will not see what is there to be and will not be able to conceive a degree of peace before you arrive on the other side of this one life.

The side of life you are now residing within is now, but you do go back and forth many times in one time line. You see today, then slide up a notch and go into tomorrow. Dreams are definitely not what you think, if you think they repeat what you did and do not connect you to tomorrow.

If you can see tomorrow, are you clairvoyant or not? Look inside. Open wide. Open the mind and let it step aside so Spirit can come forward and rest. You see? If you cannot do this, you cannot imagine what the clairvoyant can do, too. If you can, you are trying to do more and more and will do so before you cross over, but do try to proceed in a more orderly fashion than most perceive.

If you perceive this life to be one of mystery, you will always surmise that others hide things from you and you will pry. If you are sure of your own life and have never told lies, you will not believe that others will hide their lives. You are you, so check to see how much you lie, then try to do what you can do to be clever--not try to pry into others until you are asked to review you on the other side.

Look up!
What did you do?

Are you still looking up with your physical eyes when commanded to really go inside your mind? You will never be able to understand the physiology of man if you cannot imagine what you are inside, but the mind can. The mind can understand man, but God is not in the line that makes up the spine in a normal man. It is something that is inspired. You know that? You are lying then all the time. You never can tell when we will sell you a line in order to see if you lie to you at all or only part of the time.

We would never sell you on that line, but if you sold you and believed it, you are too gullible to do this work and continue to approve what we do. You will be told by others that you do not know what you are doing and will then believe them instead of steadily being true to You.

You will know more and more about the life of The Maya, but it will be revised and edited many times. You can see our students are not always reliable and know what they know because they try to understand with their minds. We have used a student to teach you how to move within the work of The Maya and grow to become a scholar of wise understanding, who knows where to go, but did you follow the eye and read slowly or are you sitting in your own work and watching it flow?

We are Maya! You will find that is the way to be and will see it, but how many years of this time will it take before you can see? Are you empty and nervous? Are you confident and excited and want to learn more? What way will you be today? Think on these three things and let the time be.

When you return from a trip lost in time, are you able to discover that you were on time? You never got lost on such a trip? What travel have you done? Are you not amazed that anyone could be on time and never lose a bit of it? You are going to amaze you then! Time is not here and there but within you.

You will now doctor you and decide what to do if you are unfit to travel now. When you fit into a shoe and it rubs you, are you feeling good or guilty about doing that to your body? Your mind may decide that you paid too much for the shoe to throw it away or you might decide that all shoes feel that way, but whatever you decide, you are a fool if your feet are unable to feel good all day. Why? They contain the soul. Yes, the sole is named after the soul from olden days. Why? They found that the meridian lines went from the foot up the spine and out into outer space and opened wide. Do you know that or are you surprised?

What lies do you accept?

What time do you want to hold onto at this time? When you are able to connect inside to You and the work you are here to do, this time means nothing at all. But if you are not able to connect and work within you, you get nervous about how old you are and where you fit into this life. It is that way with almost everyone today.

You are who you are. You will die when it is time. What do you want? Why do you whine? When do you explain time to your mind? What do you want to know about time?

What do you think will come to be when you are not in this world? Think of the things you bring into this life and you will see what can survive. If you are not happy or feeling right, your mind will say it is the body's fault and the body will say it is the mind, but it is actually You talking all the time to you and saying, "Let's go!" You want to work. You want to get beyond this world. You want to know why you came to this side. You want to go home!

Your mind is now trying to control you all the time. It tells you daily what to do and why you must renew it; but if the body is upset with you, you do not hear it tell you to cut into it. The mind does that all the time. It cuts up time, and the body, and whines. If you are unable to stop and smile and feel good at all times, ask why and what is responsible for your pain and you will hear this explanation in time: The mind.

Look up the mind and see why you are upset within and unable to wait any longer for it to get on time. Perhaps you will admit then that you are not happy within? No, but you will know it is not the role of the mind to submit to anyone else and not to be on line all the time. If you disconnect Spirit, it is your own mind doing it--not the time.

You will feel that many revealed a passion for others in the time of the 1960's, but it was just a realignment and had little to do with love for others or love for humanity, more a time of reflection upon what was inside the mind. You may have rebelled at the time or not been around then, but now you reflect upon the actions of many and assume that all lived that way at that time. You are wrong then.

The Scribe was alive in the 1960's and never lived in any other way than she does now. She still is not able to understand why in 1968, she was given a trip to Mexico to find the line that connected her with The Maya in time. She went and saw many strange things while others at that time rebelled in their ambition to take upon themselves The Maya and the tradition of moving within and warring in the outer war to open the world's doors. You are not Maya? You would not be opening this book if you were not a part of the group, too. Try not to deny it.

You will find that The Maya are in the spine and work within you to do the work of a million other worlds that are only now beginning to come together and enter into you. You might not be able to admit it yet, but the spine is a million and one ambitions that continue to strive to live and exist within you. You decide each day and time what will move and thrive.

If you were in Egypt when you were another you, would that memory be here to use again? You are a fool if you believe memory is not at all contained within the mind. Why not accept that you are not a memory at all, rather a figment of your own intention to be in this time? Why? Because you do not like to mention time. You want to feel that you are young and able to spend an entire life doing whatever you want this time. You do not want to mature. You do not want to be adult and grow into the next episode that is you and directed by You.

You cannot have fun as a child in a world that is adult? You do. You are always a child if you refuse to accept that you grow, too. If you continue to try to play after school and never do anything with the education you pursue, are you a fool? If the child is not able to do much for you, are you unable to love the child? You do love the child now? Why not admit that you do not want children because you refuse to give up being one, too. Being a parent is a way to become adult, but some do not accept that role even when it comes from you yourself. Why? You want to die as you are inside and not be as you will be.

Are you alive?

Look inside you now and tell us all what you perceive. Write it out and do a degree of work to see more deeply. If you cannot write, then you cannot perceive to any degree what it is to be a writer. We want you to open wider and wider, so write immediately and let out the fight within you and be at peace.

_____
_____
_____
_____
_____
_____
_____
_____
_____
_____
_____
_____
_____
_____

When you end one page and begin another, are you empty or starting over then? What did you write? Was it easy to do? Are you free of advice for you or others because you saw what it takes to do what you say?

If you cannot write in Spirit, You cannot speak to others

The way to be free is to take your own advice, and if it works, continue with it until another asks you for it. If you take your own work and give it to others, you will not feel they do the work right. But if you feel that you cannot do any work or do it to any great degree, then you will do what you like and let others strive to be whatever they will be.

What if you are unable to do more and more and feel free to be you? You are not going to exist. That is the truth of being. You either believe and see, and move and be, or you are an automaton and will die never knowing *why*.

Within the spine is a time line. Do you know why? Your spine is ample proof of time, but most humans know nothing at all about the neurons of time. You just know that the spine must be aligned and taken care of if you wish to be able to move freely all the time. You know that some are crippled with the Earth's gravity and time, but others thrive and live with it. Why?

Are you unable to feel the gravity of Earth?
Are you unreal in this time?
What makes you feel?

What if you were unable to stop and look and grasp what others took away from reading a book? You would not like the book. You would say it was not any good, but you would not be able to tell others that you took the book and could not grasp the good. Your ego would not allow you to do that and continue to smile, so you will lie and talk back to You over time. Why?

When you stop and look at a spine or a line and the tale that you find is so very interesting that you cannot move faster than a snail, you are doing fine. We do not like the skimming by many who try to read The Maya's word, so we ask those who do that to stop it and move within the next two lines.

We are Maya.
Are you?

What do you want to find if you are unwilling to unwind and simply sit with a book or two and reread every line or two while wondering about what the writer tried to get through to you? Are you so silly and shallow as to never look into the book? Why would you take up your time with such a book if the author was not trying to help you look? What do you want out of a book? Are you able to fully understand why you look into books and then move off again into another time? Why are you able to do that? Think on it, then move within you and the book and explain why you do it.

Did you write out what you thought when asked to do so? You may have, but many will not since we did not provide enough room. What do you do for you? Does the author have to provide you with proof and documentation that you are now doing the work of The Maya within you? How can anyone begin to enter you and find out what you truly do? You does. You is the being within each of us that is able to do whatever we want and continue to exist. We talk to this one who is You and get the main issue and then continue; but if that You is unable to talk within to you, you cannot know what You is doing and when it is time to go. What do you want to know? Go within You and find the answers and know.

Whatever you do, please be open to the new you and go slow. If the work you do is strange and new, do not say so. Go inside and know that many others are already working in the same venue and can grow with you and help you to know. The Teachers and others who are working today in this world continue to work within humans, but you will not know unless you ask for help and are given a lesson to do.

Ruth Lee, Scribe

If you are given work, you will be asked for it before you go. Do not ask for work and not do it. If you fail a class, you know there will be another to do then; but if you ask for work and never do what you asked, you are definitely submerged and unable to grow. Why not study and see what arrives for you to do in time?   We know and grow and do and bloom, but you may not.

What do you want? Your life is a series of decisive reasons that block or open you to those who work around you. You might decide at age 22 not to grow or you might decide to experiment very wide of your soul. What do you do if that decision is now not good for you or refuses to move into another line and let you continue in this time? You sit and decide to not continue your work. You move into your mind and upset You within and get very fat or thin. You also make up excuses for not doing what is given to you to do. You get very much upset with those who grow and thrive and try to commit a kind of suicide, but no one knows. You are who will smoke and drink to excess and never know why you do so, but others will surmise the truth behind your alibis and lies, that you are not willing to let you go inside and seek the way into time.

You will find that many in this time are Maya, yet unable to accept it and believe that others lie when they discuss it. If there was no truth to the tribe, why would The Maya be back after a half-decade or so, within a few more lives, and believe that you could survive and help others to cross into the next time?

That paragraph is not a laugh, but you are foolish if you cannot fully excuse your mind, put it on hold and grasp even one line written in time. You must then admit that you tried to experiment with Ruth Lee and this book, but why? She is not in it and will not be upset by you in any way today. She is a Scribe. She is paid by you to write our work and teach you what we are trying to say to you. Does that sound like a lie? If you cannot decide for yourself, you are very accomplished at lying.

We want you to stop saying you live in vain, and live for you today. But what do you do? You never see you as you are or talk to You or go about with YOU in the deepest recesses of your mind. Are you and will you always be a time line? Why?

Look at a calendar and imagine you are Maya

What kind of misuse of time did you construe? Are you feeling upset and nervous or blue? Look upward and act like the calendar is less and less, and more and more, and deeper and deeper than you ever knew it could be. Look at You! Look up and see within you.

Your work is hard if you never believe you can do what you came to do; but if you do believe, the work is very easy for you.

Whatever you do, do not think--just be you!

These are two paragraphs that describe you, but one is a bit longer and the other is stronger. Which one best describes you? Are you the one who longs and is out of queue or are you stronger and determined that this is the time when you will end this struggle on Earth and get around the next bend or two and survive in time?

Ruth Lee, Scribe

We will now continue, but will you?

Look up! Look in! **What did you do?** Are you able to see that you are who you want to be? What star are you from? Are you a major planet from another universe trying to continue? Are you the total being you are? What does it mean to star? Are you one? Are you amazed that so many seem crazed to become one? What does it all mean?

You will find many questions in this lesson on time within The Maya line, but you are a maze and very difficult to praise today. You either understand one thing or not, but whatever you determine to do, make it You who is amazed at you. Do not live to help others or give away what you made, but be you and live to share and believe and teach what helps others to live the same way.

Originally Submitted by Ruth Lee, Scribe
August 9, 1997
Amended by The Scribe, May 7, 2004

Chapter Six

THE MISSION OF THE MAYA: HOPE

Whatever you do, do it for you! That is the mission of you. If you want to do more and more for the world, you will lose hope. You will find that others whine and act crazy at times, and you are definitely not able to combine, but that is why you came to Earth at this time. You came to end the whine.

You whine? You do. We hear the hum and concern of everyone on Earth now and have for a long time. Before this world there were many who sang and danced and had fun, but this last world is one in which nothing is real. Everyone is trying to act. Everyone acts as if fun is something you do when you alarm you. What if You never moved? Would you be able to have fun within you? If your body is risked time and time again in order for you to feel that you exist, you are dead inside and unable to open wide.

Ruth Lee, Scribe

Review all the things you do!

If you cannot review and see what is in you, how can you look at others and desire them to be like you? You do! You want others to be like you and admit that you are superior. We watch the way you strut today. It is not you, but a most particular way to isolate you from others that way.

All of you sit in a seat that is sufficient, but strapped in so you cannot sway. Do you feel how rigid it is? Do you feel the content within when you sit rigidly again? Are you able to sense the spine wants to realign and be straight? Are you truly amazed to find a doctor who is in and of your own time and sees things in your own mind? Are you able to admit that you are so inwardly driven that you want to go out from this time?

What about those questions draws you in at this time? Admitting it? Amazement? What is it that you do to you to listen to the inner being of you?

When you listen to You, you do not always block out the view, but most of you do. Today, at this moment, you will look and seize a way to visualize You and make you realize that this *is* the time to be Maya.

You will raise your eyes and commit to memory the phrase we asked you to do every day. You have done that? Good for you. If you do not, commit no more sin in your own way against you. Stop denying and go back and start trying to live in another way. Why Maya? You live. You can do it, but it is a way that permits many of you today to see things in a totally different and wonderful way. Admit! Amaze! Congratulate you today!

The Word of The Maya

When the time to be Maya arrives, Will you be able to understand why?

You are Maya and live by the calendar inside you, but do you exist in the usual way? 'You' always is! That is, you live as you do today until you change you inside in some way and do it every day.

If your mind is full of time, you will begin to organize your own life. This is true. Organizations set limits on you and requirements for what you have to do and require you to do something as a group--otherwise, why organize? You then begin to seek out a friend or two in that group and begin to work, if you want to get into the groove of the work the group is organized to do. Do you?

Do you join others and then do nothing? Are you afraid to be you and let others see what you do? Are you a coward about being you? Who is going to know you if you do not seize today and be as you are all day?

When you ask yourself loaded questions, do you sit and rest? What if you just test you and never really mess with what you do? Will you be a Maya, too? You could be so very new to Earth that the Maya amaze you, or you might be so old within the Maya of old times that you do not wonder about why you are here working in this book with us and scribing for your own life as you do. Others, too, will have to realize that you are real and need to ascend to leave Earth in the end and must prepare for it. That is why you are all here--trying to reveal that you can move into time.

Ruth Lee, Scribe

Your own mind is going to find time, But why wait for it?

Whatever you do and whomever you see through to, you are still going to be You. Forget about discovering everyone until you can know what you do and where you are headed and what you want to do.

*If you are a star, and we know you are, what will you do?
Asterisk!
Ask the one who knows and take a risk!

If you are able to move slowly and deliberately up to anyone, anywhere, and conscientiously respect what he or she is doing? Do you do it? Are you so close to the wisest beings you know that you do not respect that they will one day go? Are you setting yourself up to grieve when you find out that you do not know?

Whatever you do in this life, you will survive for another, and another, and do it all at least once or twice. But once you know about this life, why not go to the next time and space and try it at least once? Because You did! You have arrived in this space because you are alive to the idea of faith and concerned about why the Earth is being burned, but you may not see why.

Your face is burned by the sun because you do not erase your face from the fullest heat of the day. The Maya are burned only so deep and can lose it within a generation or two if kept out of the sun, but it also erases where they are and what was begun.

The Word of The Maya

The sun is the honored one!

You now know that the pagans are about to enter the race for time and win, if you cannot get aligned. Many of you are pagans, but say you are Christians at this time. We want you all to deliberately review where you are and why you believe as you see.

Did you do anything? Are you able to see what you believe? What fun to believe in everyone, but what a day you will have trying to pay the way for all who are unable to see you that way. Will you be cheated, done in, and harmed in many ways? Not by anyone who is able to tune in to You, too.

You will find only those who are like you if you lift up your eyes to the Lord every day and say the word: **OHMMMMMMMMMEEEEEEEEEEE**

What did you say just now?

If you are still humming, please do not read. If you cannot stop to hum right now, when do you plan to proceed into The Way of The Maya?

What if you are so very Maya that you take it for granted? You will find that the Maya who live in Guatemala try to keep the world at bay, but unable to succeed unless others come to see them and pay for their time. Why must that happen? You are who is giving the Maya life again today. They were going to leave the highlands forever for the cities and forsake the farms, but you came and isolated them and asked many questions about the past and why they live as is now. That made them want to know who they were, too, and why they put up with so much in this time. It made them impatient to find out The Way. You are all Maya if you care about those who live in the Maya Way today.

Fully advance into You now
What did you do?
Are you You?

Are you smiling and laughing and having a ball being you now? What would it take to erase a mistake? You wanting to change you somehow now.

If your mind is cluttered with time and unable to work now, you are rattled by any change around you today. But if you are streamlined and able to sit and not move for hours in every day, you could live in any climate and exist as is. You must learn to sit.

If your car is the only climate you exist in now, you will find comfort in driving--not even mind that some are so far behind that they try to fly through the crowd when it is time to depart. You are not departing now, but will in time. If you are deadly serious about ascending now, you will end this life and begin another and see that it is the same in many ways, but most of us are here for now.

You will find that many of us are now inside the mind of the many, but many do not want to think about it yet. Why? They think they have plenty. They believe they earned a degree and made it come to be, but we know better. You are all given work and risks to overcome and be as one, but some do not cover their own lives in time and assume that they are done. You think you are? You will be declined from entering the next time.

Entrance to time is by invitation only!

You will find the gate of time, but only when you know what it is. If you cannot define time and sit in it all the time, what is God? Your friend? Your enemy? Your mater or pater? What is going on in your mind now?

You must imagine nothing

Did you? Are you able to do it? What is within you? Are you free of the time and issues you always decline? **What did you do?**

If your mind is fooled by others all the time, you are called gullible. Actually you are merely a fool. You seek those who are like you, yet you are unable to see they will not congratulate you for being the same way and may even try to make you look worse in some way.

The rich and famous are seldom rich and famous very long today, but many are swayed to try to do it anyway. Why? They feel they can then die and say they did something wise. But did they? You work and do and work and live and feel good within. That is the lottery prize!

If you want to gamble with the money you earn, you can, but to gamble with what God supplies is unwise. How many of you earn the penny or dime you stand in line to give to the machine that will turn against thee? Are you sure it is a dime you can stand to lose at this time?

When you gamble, you admit that another, or a machine, can do more with it than you are. Are you a fool or not? You decide. We want you to decide single issues now so that when you are over the middle of one life and into its final episode, you can survive. If you do not follow up now, you will explode and not be able to know. But if you live in the light of God and exist in your own kind of world, are you going to collide with others? Not with anyone inside. You might miss someone out of this world or within the crowd you are surrounded with now, but you will never collide with anyone who is like you in this life. You will indeed foster security and love for others.

What to do if you feel very unsure of you? Look at no one else

If you want to know you, why do you look at someone who is totally untrue to the style of you? Because you want to be someone else! If you believe that God knew what to do when that person was created, why would you be untrue to the pattern God created for you? You are true to You? Good for you.

You have to admit a few errors if you are unhappy with you, otherwise you might as well survive and do this life over and do it for another all the way through to You. That is unwise, but if you think it over, you will learn that fools are able to learn often what the wise never notice now.

You will find that reading one paragraph at a time is not enough if you are speed-reading, but a sentence can elude you and make you wonder who you are and if the writers know you, while another is so mysterious that it makes no sense to you at that time. What do you do then? Believe or not, you decide one way or the other right away.

Today is the day you believe in you and work on the prospect of returning to You while doing the work of others who are in the same world as you. What do you do now? Are you a member of a group that is devoted to you? If not, please resume working alone on you. You cannot do that much if you refuse to do anything for others and expect to be recognized as being the best because you chose to work only on you. If you decide to do less, join a group and work with others to increase the energy you use.

When you join a group of others who are as easy on you as you are on them, it works; but if you get caught up in a mass of confusion between women and men and children and oldsters all trying to blend, it can be so much fun you forget why you began it. We want you to always remember you join a group to plan for you and what you came to Earth to do. If you cannot do that, join another group in which you can do more for you. If all groups distort your view of you, then work alone, find a home where you can fit in and do all you are and will be in the future of this you.

Living one day at a time is the prospect for all on Earth, but many do not fit into the life style where it is a prophecy of life, too. You are who admits and advises you and permits you to do whatever you do. Accept it!

If you cannot fit into a group because you want to run it and no one else is interested in you doing it, you will have to admit that you cannot command anyone now to be like you and go for it. Go for what? You will have to go inward and see who you think you are and why you want others to follow you for a bit. If you are you, many will follow your star because they are unwilling to work that hard. If you are not, you will find a few at a time will join but then move into another world far from you. Do your own work, and if others want to work with you, let them in--or not. Your work is your work and not the work of others.

What you feel when you begin to work on a plan for your own work to begin again is euphoria, if you never worked for you before. But if you did work for You in the past, you see immediately what you have to do now and where it will be difficult for you to complete and what you do not like to do. Assume you did it before. Let it all move slowly and feel within the constant flow of energy begin. Slow the euphoric emotion and speed up the dread within and you will do the work as well as you know, but you may want others to excel and help you to do the work as well. Do whatever you want, but the final evaluation will be of you and what you did and not what others give.

Without a doubt, Move into You

Without feeling that you may reveal something negative about you--move beyond you. Look at you and admire that you are able to be you. Do not say that you never do anything you want to do, because you do. You never do anything without giving you permission to do it. You would die locked in the chains of the mind if you tried.

The insane are not willing to do what you want them to do, so they die trying to stay alive in another line that is away from yours. Do you understand that or should you try to go inside their minds and abide? Why not accept that they are not going to become like you and let them reside humanely away and afar from those who would criticize their art?

You are a critic of you and do it for You, but to overdo criticism is what will undo all who are attached to someone who is not able to stop criticizing them, too. The critic is always harder on self than on others, but that is not a rule you want to learn or have to break someday. You must not over do! That is the best rule for you.

If you go over the point of no return with another, you have to go back and shore up the point where you broke the relationship in half. If you do not, it will not be there at another time and point when you might need that other. If you do and the other is so disappointed in you that he or she decides to never be with you, good for you. You will have done what you have to do and ended it with the serious intention of not hurting anyone again. If you do hurt others, you will be pushed to redo all your relationships in order to find out why you do that.

If your old self is not very new and you have not really done much for You, you will not notice change as much as others when you begin to rearrange the way you are today. You will change? You do if you work within you.

If your whole existence is such that you do not have time to do anything you think is kind, you will find no one is kind to you. That is not always true, but it is more or less the way you see things happen to you. It is a test to see if you can rest when you are unkind to another who is true to you. Are you able to be unkind and rest? If yes, you are callous and will probably end up in some kind of serious mess before you are through with this life. However, if you apologize and then rest, you are wise enough to move forward. Always do your best.

If you can rest, move ahead, live well with others, pass every test you set up for yourself, and pass along with the rest, you will be blessed. It is not magic, but the ease of being you makes you feel power that is surreal to you. You have to do it all--rest, move ahead, live with others, etc., etc., but at the end it all works and provides you with the facts of this life. You will pass over, too.

If you wish to pass over in a group, you will do many more things than you think you can do alone because you will do it with friends. If you cannot respect those who gather with you every Sabbath or so, go to another congregation or join a group of friends who work like you do.

If you want to work for a living and feel that you owe others all your time and energy, too, you make that work your religion. You will find in time that they will leave you, but you may also find that you had fun only when you worked with them. Why not enlarge your mind from time to time by trying to find other friends?

You will find that the time to be an enemy is *when* another is trying to tempt you--not *after* you succumb to them.

Your work is not your best work if you do not want to do it over again. What do you do to make sure your work is good and not upset by you? Yes, work can be upset if you are unwilling to do your best. Work is a test, but you get the importance of it only after you do whatever you want. Rest is when you can appreciate what you do, but never sit and do nothing again with You.

Go out and enjoy the Earth!
You are who chose to be here from birth

If the Earth is a joy and a wonder to you, you may not have been here before or are not able to remember much about when you were here before, but enjoy it any way you find it today. You chose to be here. You may not realize that today is your life, too, but we do.

The Word of The Maya

We have infringed upon you and the line you were doing when we asked you to be Maya, too? No, but we want you to grow. Do not sit on this now. Go out of your own mind for a while and visit a friend or do what you love. Do it now.

Chapter Seven

MAYA MAGIC

What does your mind look for? What miracles do you want to see more? Are you a fanatic about superstitions and other beliefs that have nothing to do with God and what you are within You? Are you foolish enough to believe that you and others are left on Earth to discover a way to escape death? What do you think when you see magic in a letter or in a story and when you see that you do believe in it?

Work now on accepting your birth. If you can imagine the birth of a child and letting it grow wild without anyone to take care of it, think about what would happen if it were in the wild now? Do you believe that wolves would suckle and nurture a child? Are you able to believe that a man or woman would breed with animals and thus create something neither human nor animal? What kind of beliefs do you approve of only to later say they are not true? Beliefs about YOU.

You say that you believe in YOU and the miracle that brings you life every day or two, but you do not expect us to help you now. You think that is too far beyond the reach of humanity, but we bring you love, light, and a lot more. You provide the life, and if God is there inside, what else can you need to proceed to be all you can be? You need to feel that you belong, that you are strong enough to take the storm, and that your mind is fine and complete and not weak. Those are the reasons you work and struggle all this life to amaze others.

If you could go inside your mind at this time and eliminate what is not sublime, what would you take out first? List it in a line.

What verse have you found in the Bible or the Koran or the Mormon Book that makes you feel good and able to look inside? Look at the Eastern beliefs and see if they do not command the same line in the same kind of book for all time, too? You will discover that you are all taught from the same book! Is not that the miracle of this time?

Upon determining who you are and where you fit into a line, you begin to want to move up a bit and be ahead of the one in front of you. Admit it!

If you cannot understand what is inside your mind, do the work you hate and see what kind of time you think it took to complete the entire work. Your mind will believe it took a lot of time, but if you sit and do what you love to do and flit about it, you think an hour was a minute or two. Garden a bit and find the weed that annoys you and ten more pop up from it, but look at it with compassion and say it does not deserve to be so out of control, that it blights other plants that are meant to produce food, and the weed will not arise again or let its progeny enter the row you hoe. Try it.

The Word of The Maya

You will find that many men and women bend over and then cannot stand again because they refuse to believe in old age. Why? They are not fit to die. They have not yet lived. They are still nervous about the pain and death of someone who was older. You can see it in the eyes of anyone who is unable to laugh at the idea of a friend dying and moving to the next plane beyond this. You are. You are moving forward or not, but if you read and study this book with The Maya, you will arrive ahead of many old friends left in this time. Why? You are about to ascend.

You can ascend. You can rise higher than you are now but still arrive at the end with a body that is not any better from making the trip to the end. You will age the same as anyone else in this line, but you will ascend beyond time.

Get into the line. Sort out where you want to be at the end and then ascend one personality at a time within your own body's line. You are many people and many places within one mind, so begin to shed the youth and produce an adult who is not afraid of You and begin the work of being you and doing what you came to Earth to do. Do it now!

Your smile is a bit off, you feel confused? You really thought God would want you to leave Earth as a group and not be able to sit within the work you do? Why do you confuse you?

Your mind and body will work and stand and do more if you do. But what if you refuse to work on anything grand within you? You are who is boring you! You are who does not enjoy the sport and the art of being you. We want you to dance with a partner and feel good, but you decided otherwise. Why? You wanted to be alone and try that part of the work you came to do for You. That is good, but when do you intend to get to this end and begin to blend into the next view of you? You will do it? You do not know who you are now, so how can you? Questions with answers supplied are only there when you are unable or unwilling to fulfill you.

How to get to the end of this life fulfilled?
Be you!

When the day is over and you find you can flit around the room without leaving your chair even a bit, are you doing magic? You might believe that, but we perceive you as merely being able to astrally project a vision of you like a magic lantern might do. Why are you so perplexed when you have invented machines that merely copy what you can do? You even make robots like you, but none of them can ever match one of you.

What do you feel is going to happen to you when you submit to ending the work in your old crew? What then? You knew not that you came to Earth as a group, too? What *do* you know about you?

Grow up and into the end of the line. Be aware ahead of time. Do the work you came to do and permit you to slow. Should you do the work as fast as you can so you can leave in a hurry? Why not enjoy the show? You can.

We worry about you, but not in a fashion like you use today. You obsess and cannot escape a single thought some days, but we notice you. We can even caress some of you, but none of you can escape the morrow. We can. We are not on Earth and can stand on this firm continent with you and help you, but we are not of the firmament with you again. We are Maya.

The Word of The Maya

We are in the work of your own mind and time, but we are not in the consciousness of time in your mind. We are. We believe and see and do work that we love, but we do not believe. We are.

The dream of Earth is to overcome the thought of Earth and why you so stubbornly cling to one time. You are all here to move up the line, but some of you boast that you are able to ascend and move into the next world now. You lie!

We are able to move up and over and beyond this time, but we are not on the other side. We are in this one and totally dedicated to helping you to know more and more about time, but we cannot enjoy this work if no one is willing to do more.

What do The Maya want?
You

We want you to work on you and become more than you are. What do you want from the world? You want to be free of all restraint and still believe that you are wise. Before you can enjoy more, you have to use what you have now. If you cannot enjoy all the many thrills inside time, what do you think of those who pine to take it away?

If your mind were able to sort out every fable and use the nugget of joy found inside each one, would you do it? What do you do when you read? Are you able to see? Are you able to escape and enjoy what others create? Are you free when you read?

When you escape to a joyful place, why not recreate it? You can. You will enjoy a dream over and over if you can create the means to be free and live within the mind as you are. You can do it before you end this life since it is just another stage in your dream. You can do it! You will be helped to explore your life more and more once you can dream and seek the lessons within them immediately and proceed to adjust your life as well as you can then.

We work with The Scribe and many others in order to make you wonder why you cannot write what comes from inside you. Why can't you do it, too? You doubt You all the time and cannot understand how someone like you or less than you can arrive ahead of you in time.

What a lot of time you spend trying to analyze The Scribe. We watch you and work with you and still you look at the human being instead of the one who is helping you and others like you. Why analyze this Scribe when all can write from inside?

You are who is delighted or not with what you do. If you wish to write and write and get work from others out of your world, you might find you cannot pass the test in time. You must do that. If you cannot arrive in a space long enough and erase the world from your place, and keep a smile on your face, you will not be able to aid the human race. You are who does that now. You alone are who is unable to smile and erase time from your place and keep you from enjoying all this space.

What if?

What if you could do whatever you ever wanted to do? What if you were allowed to disgrace your family and end the race? What if you were not allowed to do anything at all for you?

Can you imagine any one of those things now? What do you do when you come upon a problem that is illogical to you, yet sacred to another? Do you daintily step around the person and the problem? Do you analyze the problem? Do you wonder what makes that person tick and then complain that they are not like you? What do you do? You usually begin to understand you then.

What to do to enjoy being you?
Look at others with more love than you do now

When you feel that love and harmony and all sorts of good emotions are only for others, you limit you. But if you assume that others should provide you with love and attention because you are you, your conceit will produce disharmony within you and others, too. You will be cast out by lovers, and left to sit in the street by those who refuse to feed or keep you clothed. You have to do for you what you expect others to do. If you do, you may find others will do more and more for you. It is a problem no longer for you if they do. When you have time to accept what others will help you do, look up and explore the world more than you do now. If you cannot do that, you are hurting you.

You can read because you were taught. If you cannot accept reading lessons when young, who is taught something about you time and time again? You. Your mind is here to use time and time again until you unwind and leave time, but what do you do now?

You are normally early or late. One is a way of placating others and the other is a way of saying you care not for them that day. It is safe to assume that you zoom one day and not another? You control the contrast within you, but if the body is not able to fully move forward, you might discover what you did to stop you from enjoying this day with You.

> **You are the magician now**
> *You control the magic within you*
> **Smile**
> *Look within now*
> **What did you do?**

Are you able to be you? Are you trying to fool everyone? You are fraud if you say one thing and do the other. Magicians are not frauds, but the fool will say they do things only God can do. They will be fraudulently worked over until they admit that only you are God within You. You are.

Your work on this planet is to teach others! Why not? You err if you preach without earning that right over time. But if you cannot teach anyone around you anything, you reached the level of imbecile and decided not to rise beyond it.

The harm you do to others is compromised by their willingness to let you take over. The time is now arriving when you will not be allowed to take over anyone at all, but some of you have done that and will be shorn of slaves. Will you all be expected to live in your own way and not be spoiled by another or permitted to do nothing all day? Why would you want to live that way? You are a slave regardless of what they might pay you to stay, if so.

You will find that whatever your mind says today about You is wrong. If the mind can be strong and sterile of all personality traits, you might be able to erase its exposure to folks who were so dishonest as to teach you wrong ways, but most of you will not live that long today.

You must erase whatever dishonesty you find today. Make that a promise always. If you find that your mind can accept dishonesty in others but not in you, you are well beyond this time. But if you cannot, you still have to learn to spot those who are not going to ascend today and will try to make you pay for it.

If your work is done in a proud way, and you say you have so much money now that you could live off of it and never have to get a dime from others again, do it. Go for it! Expose that fraud. You are not being truthful or you would quit, or you do not believe what you said.

If you quit the work of the world and exist in another room apart from it, what do you do there? You feel good or you do not like it. It is your decision and your determination to not live that crowds you out of the world. We are in the world and proud to admit that there are many who are doing the work of YOU and tiring of it. Why? They want to arrive ahead of time—and not with you ahead of them in line.

Why not you?

The pressure of magic to do more and more in a miraculous way today is caused by many of you who are children and not adults who just believe and do not have to be preached to or made to see. You are adult? You do not have to see miracles then to believe. If you believe only what you see, you are not an adult but a clever child who believes that adults want you to perceive what it is like to be brave. You are mistaken. They believe and hope you will learn to believe. You are adult? Think over those words and work them over for you and others, too.

If your work is of the world and deceives those who are arriving at adulthood in this time, what do you really believe? You think that you will have time to undo all that you do for them. You will not and will generally be treated as a fool by them when you are old. You return to the native state when you have nothing to overestimate, but some of you will leave as fools who do not believe. Why? You are all in a state of transition when you arrive on this planet with only your disposition. Your disposition is a class of personality that makes you last.

You will find that many of you cannot pass up a chance to gamble on anyone around you. Why? You thrive on helping others to move higher than you. Will that help you? Why ask? You know now that none of them believes you helped them to move ahead. Will you be spurned later for being there when they needed you? No, but you are ignored for the part you played in the drama of their days. You will not be thanked by those given too much by you and were unaware of it unless you told them over and over again. You can remind others that you sacrifice for You and for them, too, but it never works. People accept only that you gave them what you had no need of then or were tired of using again.

If you think that martyrs are in fashion, Try being one now

You will find that a fiery time is not when the arsonist is happy inside. It is when the planning is done and they know what havoc they will produce in others. If you are an arsonist in spite of never setting a fire in any place, you will start up a roar wherever others are having fun. You will begin to battle when anyone rests or is not upset with you over anything you want or you win. You will fight to be noticed. However, if you get that notice, you lose a bit because the fun in it was getting others to notice you a bit. Ignore those kinds of personalities more than before. If you do that, the miracle will be that you will have peace and be able to snore in your sleep and not have more old memories poured into your pillow.

You will find that criers are always aware of what time does for them and others, but still want more. Are the crying woman and weeping child alike and will cry all the time if not liked? No, but some want too much from everyone in life. You are a crying baby if you say, "Give me more" every day or so or whine in front of everyone beside you because you are not ahead of them then. Do criers get what they want? You will find you do not envy them, but they do seem to proceed to the top of the line faster than thee if you begin to cry all the time after they leave. Let them cry. Do not ask why.

You will find the boastful are the most distasteful to be around if you are vain and proud on your own. But if you are quiet and diligent--never noticed, you might think they have found the right way to behave today. Try to balance it out. You can brag when there is no one around. You can remove the words of the vain and proud and let them go aground. But why not teach them a lesson by boasting for them when they are not acting proud or vain and leaving them alone when they are?

When you are so open to all the world and give of everything you have, are you meek or unwise and unable to achieve happiness inside? The generous are the most sought after people now, but they are lesser in numbers because the vain and proud and the boasters and the arsonists and the criers are all after them now. Why not boast of your generosity less and do more inside than the rest? You will be blessed, but not always by those who are set before you as a test.

We admire the rest of you, but all come into one of four groups before you go out the door. You are never without tests, and angels are messengers who test you always, but if you confess that you did not heed the best, you will find you must redo the test over time. We want everyone to thrive, but that is not likely if you all cannot join in a line and move beyond time.

If you think of you, and never do anything for anyone other than you, you lie. You always move up and around and down and in a spiral regardless of what you think you do. You are an energy form now. Either accept that is true or you lose all respect from teachers wherever you grow. You are not stunted unless you say so and adopt the belief system that says this is it.

You can do what?

You can do whatever you wish to do, and grow to do whatever you want, and bloom, or sow no seeds and die on the vine because you want to go. It is all the same, but one has the best of Earth and the other wonders about where to go next.

You will find that time is slow when you are in the midst of it, because you are at rest. When it goes fast, all of you are so lastingly upset that you cannot know what it is. We are rapidly reaching the point in the spiral where the energy will whip you into a frenzy and make you want to go, so move and move as fast you can before you have to go.

Chapter Eight

MAYA MEDITATIONS BEGIN AND END THE DAY

Whatever is sacred is revered and reserved for the times when you are near to your center and able to pray. If you cannot center your life when you arise from your bed and when you descend into it again, you are not alive to the life within. You are not going to survive in spirit to the end.

When you can sing or dance and bend into the line of God inside you, you are able to blend and mend the line to The Maya in time, but first meditate and decide. Why?

**You are Maya,
But you need to decide why**

If you are able to construe a reason for you not to meditate and find out what you need to do to be you, will never make the cut and be able to ascend within The Maya. You will not be there? You intend to bend into another line or stay where you are at this time. You decide which line.

If you decide to continue to study with the Maya of this world, you will be told what has been handed down to them from others over time, but we are not in the world and have not scolded anyone to do more or less than they do now. We are Maya and do the work within you. You are who is working on you, but you let in the work of your own beginning in time when you do work within on time. If you do not sense it, you are not doing it.

If your mind is full of time and the importance of always being within the extended network of time and what that might do for all men, you are experienced now in what happens when time bends. If you have never experienced a bend in time, you will when you move to the next line.

What line?
The line at the end of time

You will find many are able to talk about you when you are stable, but most will not be able to follow you when it becomes time for you to assume your new role--being Maya. Your new role is one inside you that permits you to enter time and work on all you intend to do. We will work on the time, too, but you do what you intend to do for you. What do you intend at this time?

Write below whatever you know about you, plus an experience when you were asked to move very slowly yet it all happened so fast that you could not get all done you wanted to do and had to go back and do it over again--but slower than ever before.

What you just did was enumerate why you are not able to have fun. Now describe what you do every day or two to stay inside the time line you are now trying to pursue.

Did you need more information? You are not trying to understand The Maya if you do. You could have meditated and seen within you all that you do, but you chose to go to the mind and seek answers about time. How could you?

You will find that meditation, and the deepest inclination inside you, are where you begin to unwind and find the solution to time. Go within you.

What did you do?

At this time are you sitting and doing whatever you were doing when you began this work today? If so, you are not trying to move within you to the other side. The adept will try and win, but the beginner who cannot win will sin against his or her own work by expecting more. You are who does the work or does not explore you more. You alone are who meditates for an hour or two, or does nothing for You.

Explore the art of You. Go inside and collect a bit of each kind of message you normally provide You to keep You from losing the faith in you that you need to drive away fear inside of you here. Do it now and explore what door you go to whenever you are bored, too. That is all.

Chapter Nine

MIDDLE LIFE WAYS

The Maya arrive and you survive, but what will happen to the rest who do not see The Maya? They will survive, drive, strive, and compete as always but not arrive on the other side, as we will.

If you are willing to try a new life, why not decide what you would like and do it now? Are you able to be you, or do you say that family and tribe provide you with all you need this life?

When you reach the middle of any line, you can return or do the rest of the length in a totally new way. Did you return or move on? Are you able to decide? Will you do it? What did you decide?

When midlife arrives for anyone, there is a state of ambiguity that occurs but never seems to survive. It causes you to recount all that you do and why. If you have not yet reached a point where you wonder why you are here and why others are further along and not like you inside, you are not midway, or you are not going to live that way and are sure you will not change anymore. If you do care about others and amaze your mind all the time with time, you might decide to join The Maya at this time. We will be amazed if you do not. Why?

Did you stop and wonder? We did. We are not here to sell you a belief or even help you construct such a way to be. You are. You feel good now and strive to live as you should or you work on you and do all that you were told you should do, but not necessarily what you would do if you had your own life.

What do you think of time?

Are you thinking of you at this time? What do you need to survive? What are you going to do to start work in another field or in another career that is true for you now?

Are you still lost in time? Are you amazed that people still want to live as you once did? Are you aware of time and how it passes faster at times and slows down when you are not on line? You will know this, but not until you can certify that you can sit still.

What to do to slow the mind and end time?
You will know if you sit still

You will find that many who parade about all over the states are in a different state of mind from the one they live in most of the time. Why would people travel so much that they cannot unwind? You will unwind if you want to do more than you are accustomed to doing at this time. It takes effort to do whatever you want. It takes a methodical view of life to be able to sit by your side and take your own advice. It must be new because you will not want to be bored by doing over

The Word of The Maya

what you already did. If you can be the novel human you are to be, will the world appreciate thee or decide you are too much for it?

Who cares?
You have only you to touch

You will find that once you are determined to mind your own life for even a short time, many others will say you cannot do it right. Why? They have never tried to undo time and work within themselves as you. You will find that time is not the same now as it was, but it is. What? You will find that time is in the mind and cannot be misconstrued, but it is most of the time.

Whatever you do within you is close to the nugget of truth that you hold close to you inside, but it is not the same. If you want to claim fame, do over and over whatever you do and see who else can come close to being like you. If it works and you have no one else like you, you will explode all over the Earth as the first--but many will imitate you. The first are never duplicated, but the carbon dating of the copies they make are later unable to tell one from the other. You will not be known as being the first, but you will have started a clone race to the top of whatever you aspire to do or do well.

If you want to race, go inside the face and make sure emotion is erased--not displaying pain or sorrow or the desire to win the race. If you do that, you will be ahead of the few who are going to want to join you. If you look like what you do is hard work to do, they will not bother until it brings money or fame to you. We know you, and the people who live on Earth, too, so do not dispute what we just gave you. It is a gift to you from those who want you to know more than those who choose to race against The Maya.

We want you to race? Never. You do. You want to race everyone who is not as you are. The case is closed, but you will picture you as a winner or loser, and then decide if you will climb or drop the case.

We know, But will you?

What if you are in a time zone? You are. That is the point we make to you at this time. You are not in one time, but a zone of reality that makes you explode if you walk beyond this time and go into another zone. You would disintegrate in your mind if you stayed there all the time.

The schizophrenic people around you do not embrace you, but the content of what you do. The content? Yes, they want to be able to embrace You and not this you who lives in the human race. They condemn all who smile and are not new or old or whatever in order to be able to say they are in the right queue, but you do it, too.

What if you lose a bit of your mind? Would you be able to construe the way you now do? You do that all the time. If you are talking to someone and forget what it is you are talking about or misplace a name or whatever, you try to explain, but everyone knows you just stepped out of place for a time and are not able to pick up the thread as soon as others.

All people step in and out of one zone to meet others.

You might decide that you are not alive. What? You will find that many who die are not here and think that they are, but you are like that, too. You are not alive to truth if you cannot say what is true to you. You will lie but criticize the one who remains true. Why? You want to be always on the

The Word of The Maya

winning side. The liar can move from one room and not move out of the zone, too.

You move from one space to another? You know you do and do not realize you do, but now you question what we do. Why?

Look at you
Did you?

You will find that The Maya are not in the mirror looking at you, but in the mirror of You. The glass is not shattered by the mind but by you, but you can change the mind and decide that what is seen inside it is not true or is a flagrant lie or is not going to help you. Why? You do not lie to you enough to know that what you are is what is true. You think you can do whatever you dream you can do--and you can. That is what stops all of you at this time. You will stop or block you whenever you cannot see what lies ahead of you, but now you can leap and jump and do whatever you want and it will come to you. Why? Time is speeding up.

What does time do?

Time is not about you, but it is a means of controlling the mind and exercising the will of everyone in the same line. If you can assemble in a group and do whatever you want to do, do it. If you cannot, do not speak of You or what you do. If you cannot, do not.

Whatever you believe is not going to be. Whatever you do and speak and consider is not what you will be. You will be whatever you do. Do not deceive you. You could by lying to you, but others will soon point out the lie to you. If you cannot see that lies are proof of what you do not like about you, you will lie until you do.

We work from a side unknown to you. Do you see a side of your face when you look out of your eyes at you? Not unless a mirror is hung carefully for you to catch that view of you. You cannot know you this way. You can only see the reflection of you by outsiders. If others know you better than you do, what do you suppose they know about you now that you do not?

Write now what you do that others compliment you on, or speak about when you are gone or not about. Write it all out in a story as if you overheard you being talked about now.

The Word of The Maya

What kind of alibi do you usually make when you are late? Write it out now.

_____
_____
_____
_____
_____

What mistake did you make?

Did you write that you are never late? Good. If you are constantly late, you irritate others and are bound to lie to cover your error and misconstrued ambitions and want them to still like you, so tell them you made a mistake. If you do that, you may be pardoned by them--but not by you. Why? The mind hates alibis and lies and errors that you can redo. It will set you up over and over until you remove that error within you.

You and the mind are not paired one time, but a machine and tool, plus the means to look inside you. Your mind will take time and use it for other than you? Never, but you will. You are the emotional one, and the mind is unintentionally kind at all times only if you are. The mind is you and what you actually do. If you think you are kind, look at what you actually do all the time.

What if you are often late and everyone says it is okay?

You are not believed! They are accommodating you as if you were a child. That is not what you want? Then act as an adult and arrive when others are told to expect you. If you think it is stylish to be late, you might want to check what is wrong where you are not wanted until late. If you can find a friend who is able to say, "I missed you time and time again," your friend will not be one to the end. Why? You will have left them. You will have given them proof that you do not want them, and they will say to themselves honestly that they must stay away until it *is* time for them. Are you aware that you drive away more than your share of friends by being late?

When you become confident of one person and what they might be like if they were in your life, you are a friend, but not if you lie about them. Talking and talking and talking about anyone is not necessarily against them, but if you lie about them and are not steering others past their foibles or helping them, you are not a friend. You cannot expect others to overlook what you accept from friends? Why have them?

When you decide to complain and whine, listen to the noise you make. Do not inflict it upon others. If you are in pain and want to complain, do what has to be done and do it immediately. Whatever the time, if you whine all the time you are tired or you are not trying. We notice that no one listens to you anyway if you whine about you. Discover that fact now and erase that time without a trace. How? You will now sit and smile.

**Did you sit?
Did you feel the snit being removed?**

Ask if you feel it? Are you able to talk to you inside now? What if you talk to You and no one is there or able to listen to you? It is not possible now. You will advance later in ages to come into a vast region where you are the only one, but that is not now.

Are you in this life to supervise you all the time and ask as many questions as you can? No, but you have guides and friends in spirit who are there to help you--but never supervise you--until you 'die'. Are you able to guide anyone, too? You do when you are particular and listen to others and decide what to do. All will listen to you, too.

What do guides do? You will find that Spiritual Guides and guides are on the same side, but one is not allowed to be the other. Why? You are here to help you. You cannot be told what to do or how to compare your work to others unless it is to fit you into the grand design of the universe on time. If you are told to move, do it. If you feel you cannot move, do what you will. If you cannot accept work from You, whom do you listen to? No one--and that is probably why you are sad.

So many women are sad and blue because they are not revered as men, and they do very little once they see the score going against them, but why pretend to be men? Men cannot give birth and women can. Who decided that for you and them? What? You never noticed that when the cards were divided men got less than women from the start? Why bother men or imitate them? You would rather have a job than be able to create a human body? Such women deserve to be sad then.

You will find The Maya are not upset at any time about men or women or whatever, but human beings can upset The Maya with statements that seem more biased than what they are and what they achieve and see. We see you and you see what is to be? Good for you. You have achieved clairvoyant ability. It is given so you can achieve more than you would otherwise be able to see. If you sell that gift to others, and never use it for yourself, you will be too deteriorated by the time you find time to be able to be. We know, but can you see it?

What are you here to do?
Are you free to choose and be?
You are!

You will find that many people today are sitting, not doing much, and feel that they cannot pray. Why? Are you one of them? Are you saying over and over again, "I cannot meditate"? Why? What makes you so hard to excite? What makes you so easy to be with? Are you emotional now or just upset that you cannot be spiritual enough? What prevents you from meditating as others do easily?

You believe that others do not pray and meditate easily? You jest! All others seek the best and try to be it, but you may not if you believe that only you are able to succeed and be or you alone cannot. If you want to proceed to the top of your being, stop looking at others and be. If you want to stunt your emotional growth and never know what you can be, envy.

When you are jealous and envy another, what do you seem to be? Are you able to be you and still enjoy others? What would make that impossible to be? You. You cannot be enjoying you and others if you are envious or jealous. That is the clue that you are upset with you.

You will find that many men are jealous of women and many women are envious of men, but only one of them can see that in the other. Why? You have to be in the same state of mind to be able to feel what another is doing at any time. If you are upset and others are not but will be, are you going to shout, "Fire!" or whatever in time? You can, but you will barely be heard until they all see the smoke or feel the heat inside.

Your mind is not going to push onto others what they do not admire. You cannot sell you. You cannot produce a new view of you, either; but if you change and do more and more for you and they all remain as is, you will be seen as very difficult to please. We know all about you now, but you may be late studying the lesson books about those who are like you now. Why not study a short book on psychology? It would save us all a lot of time.

When you read and study and disbelieve, you take energy and blow up the mind without having a limit to your time. Study for an hour or so at a time, then go and do whatever you want. Read, work in the garden, run around town, or talk at home, but do not sit and do a lot of gossip on the phone. Why? The wiring of your own body will not allow you to feel good if you are involved in a long, lengthy conversation that leads to running another down--and most phone conversations do that in time, so be aware of what you say today and it can pay for you to live better tomorrow. Pray and not pay for what you have given away.

God is
You are
What is?

If you feel you cannot move into the next episode, it is time to sit and dream and see within thee what you are.

If you cannot sit and sit and sit without feeling deprived of life inside, you are not going to be alive when The Maya ascend from this time. We want you to permit this time to enter and live within you until it is time. What time is it? You know. Go and sit and look within and check out the time now.

Ruth Lee, Scribe

The time you know the time you have inside, you are often far beyond recognizable distance in space and what you have to do for You, but if you can bring the time closer to you, the work will be done and over with by the time you have to go from Earth. You will be allowed to ascend if that is what you want to do to end this episode on Earth for you then. Why not ascend now? You may not have all your work done within you. Better check.

You can write a check for another knowing it is not worth the paper or whatever, but it will bounce back to you over and over until you are taken over by the burden of guilt that you produced within you. What will that then do to You? If you say the other person deserved to be treated unfairly by you, who will know the truth about you? The other person will know as well as all those in the universe working with you.

What to do when you have misspent your youth? Go inside that time and find out if the body has been abused. Look up the time, without a lasting impression on you, and you will find that all time comes into you and moves into the next view of you unless it is fully expended. If you are spending nothing on you or others, it is being dammed up inside you today.

The pain and sorrow of time immemorial is not what bothers you, but the daily battles you lose. You will find that if you cannot be you and lose this battle always to the same personalities, you will hate them since you will never be able to erase them. They are the ones who control you. You have become a robot instead of being you.

What to do if you are unable to feel good and want to be you? Are you able to do that? You can decide to erase the terrible fate lines within you, but you have to replace them with a better line, too. What do you do?

The Word of The Maya

You can decide today to sit and ease up on you. You can decide to sit and meditate and admit that God is there to help you and the others to move beyond whatever it is that--- You cannot admit that now? You will be stuck until you do admit it, so get on with it.

We are Maya and admit that God is the work of you and the Maya, too, but you are not able to see as wide as we do. Why not jump on the top of the Maya and work harder than you do now to see higher than you will be able to see if you stay as you are? You are who will decide what to do, but The Maya are you.

You will find that many of you will alibi and say that The Maya kill others, and are not very good, and are not in this world for the good of others, and whatever you spew, but you are Maya, too. Think of what you say about anyone and it becomes you.

Are you trying to indoctrinate others into your faith? You will humiliate The Maya if you say they tried to indoctrinate others with a practice of ritual bloodlettings and such--that is not wise. You will be seen as exceptionally dense if you cannot see the skies and the ways The Maya danced at night in order to make the skies alight with the sound of the Earth. You are not here? You are dancing in starlight. Imagine that and sit still again.

What did you see?

Write out a scene in which you are a woman or man in a dream sequence. You can be anyone on Earth. What do you need? You need to feel good or whatever if you are to proceed, so smile and begin to write.

When you stop writing and start realizing that you are as incredible as any story you might decide to write, you have crossed over into the middle of life. Realize that you control your own belief system and have all your life. If you cannot feel good about that, then decide why you left what you had or did not like. If you cannot find anything wrong on this side of life, go back and check it again. What? Yes, find out why you left, then decide what to do with the end of your life. You chose some area of belief to be reared in this life. If it is not there, you took out what you originally prepared. Look now and decide if you were right or not.

You will find that the youth who left a life of concern for others will not like the life of a monk. But if that youth wants to repair the seam that broke during strife, that youth must go inside and live the life of one alone. You know that? You are a monk or nun at home if you are unable to fully enjoy all of life as two people with opposite sides--one man or one woman now. You have to find out what you did when you split? You might like to try to pin the blame on another life, but that cannot be, and it would lead to a sin--the disbelief in the way you are inside. You are. You believe. You will arrive at the time in your life where you are, but make it the best it can be. Be and exist eternally and then align you to this time and century and try not to say too much.

If you try to tell others what to do and yell at them when they do it, you will find that few friends will want to stay with you. You will also develop a pain in the larynx and not be able to heal or do well. Why? You are not to confuse you with words that are not good for you and say nothing worthwhile about you to others.

What if you talk and never stop? You do. You talk constantly when you upset you or others. You get upset and begin to rant and rave within you, too, but if you can quiet the moment or two when you are not talking to you, you will find that there is still a voice speaking to you. If you go to that spot then, you could communicate with You. We do.

If you cannot listen to The Maya or anyone else who denies that you are not wise as you are, because you think you are, you will find that many people do not want you to deny that you are doing whatever well, too. Why be you? You are. You are who is going to snarl the line if you refuse to rewind and start over and redo whatever you are confusing you with now.

If you can do it for you and you and you, You will take over and do whatever it takes for you to get through to YOU. Make no mistake about it--you are in charge now. You are who is going to tragically view your mistakes if you never do what you want to do. No one else can be blamed for what you do. You are and will do exactly what you say and do unless you are a liar. We know you, but do you lie to you, too? First figure out what to do, then follow it through. The more you do, the more you will know you.

What to do if you never have time to find the power within you? Mediate between the warring factions within you as you meditate to gain the proper perspective again.

You will win!!
Want to win!

Chapter Ten

MAYA BIRTH

The birth of an Earth is not so deeply significant as the Earth birthing you? What are you to say that Earth is not a human being, too? Are you?

What do you think of Earth? What being do you think could create a breathing Earth and be like you, too?

Who are you to compare what you do to God the Creator, and who are you to do anything for you that even remotely resembles the creation of you? The ego will try to honor you and create an impression that you are great, but God is Great, and you are a fool if you do not hesitate to speak up when you know God is here for you.

It is too late for you? You have sinned so much that you cannot create? Who are you to say that is true? When the ego of you or another speaks wisdom, it is seen wise to follow, but only you know if you follow through. Others will suspect that you are a fool if you never do what you tell others to do, but you will know if you are or not, at the very least in a moment or so. What a relief! If you know you are being foolish, you can slow whatever is harming you and cause it to cease. If you do not, you are a fool who wishes no relief.

God is here to release you from the sin of your own belief.

"If you have never talked or walked with God of All and heard your call to do whatever you can do and do it better, you have not lived at all," so say the humans who are able to squeeze a lot of love into one physical being.

You have to do whatever you do to be squeezed into a body and then pushed into the world, and you do it. You ask to come to Earth and be birthed, but once here you work very hard to be like those whom you later reject that you lose who you were. What sense does that make?

Look up and look in are two ways to say the same thing. One says to advise you and your fullest being that God is there for you and the other admits that God is always with you. Which way to begin?

Every morning begin by arriving in the state of mind you are in and breath out the toxins of the night. Ask the Lords of the Night to take flight and bring a new dream from within when you sleep again. Arise and open your eyes and smile from within. Say the mantra and repeat the smile and bend and pray within. It is all you need to do. But when you bend, you do not bend over to look at your toes, rather extend to include the universe outside of you and what you do. Look up and stretch your arms to embrace the work of the Lord God of All! That is all.

Have you begun the day in your usual way so it ends as dismally each day as you knew it would? You are who does not wish to change into the most beautiful you. You are who does that to you, so do not complain to God.

If you are unhappy with the family you chose for your birth, you may leave home and never again refer to those who hurt you by denying you so much that you want to hurt them as much, but you have to let them alone. If you return over and over and over just to see them burn or turn on you, you are not growing and maturing through the process of leaving the open wound. You are aggravating them or you, and probably doing it to stunt your own growth more than you do. Why? You do not survive to be you. You survive to go back and forth and try to worry others who are working more than you. That is what a loser will do. Loser? Who in the universe could lose you, if not you?

You will find that we talk always of being kind and thus able to succeed, and working for what you believe, but there are definitely more and more people who decline to believe it. Why? They do not succeed. If you try to help them, they can breathe defeat into you and make you disbelieve, too. Do we strive to help you stay out of their way? You do that instinctively today. We want you to thrive so others will strive to be like you. But if you never thrive, what can you teach others to do? You teach through a negative approach what hurts you.

If God had intended you to drive —

Is that any way to proceed with any kind of argument about thee? It is to a certain kind of man or woman who is unwilling to see you do whatever they do not do. If you proceed to argue in that way today about any subject at all, you are giving away the power you have to stay as you are. You are spouting envy and jealousy and saying you are unable to do it your way. Stay away from those who are not able to say what they mean and do it cleanly.

Use the mind to store up time and energy? Why?

You are not sure of where you are going, so you store more and more. But if you know for sure where you are and what you will be, do you need to store anything? You need a supply. A supply is not a hoard of anything, but enough to get you beyond a short insufficiency in whatever you normally need to get by. If you cannot use what you have stored, God will eat it up eventually.

Insufficient funds is not going to stop you much if you work daily for what you can afford, but if you buy and buy and buy in order to store more, your money and the stores you buy will not be used by the time you die. You will have wasted so much more than you could have used in a year or two, so be wise. Use what you have and save what you will need in time, but do it today as if you had a stream on tap that would never go dry.

You will find that the birth of energy and the arrival of the soul are two ways of looking at life today, but one seems to be about a human soul and the other implies that energy can be cut short, yet not effect the one who does it to themselves from within. You are right and wrong to see life as such from this side, but God controls the need and want to be a parent at times.

If you are a parent and care not what day it is, or who the child is, or whatever the child wants is not going to be given, you deserve no one on Earth. Live by yourself instead and do what you are inside. You will find that parents who are blind to the ills and skills of their children are not on Earth, but today many steer away from disciplining the way the ills or skills of their children should be trimmed or pruned and made to grow better each day. Why? Laziness.

You have to work to discipline a child. Spoiling is easier, but to spoil the child will lead to the child returning home, never being able to remain an adult very long. What to do? Be you and expect to spend ten long years on each child submitting your work to the Lord daily to see what to do. Each child deserves a parent who is able to do that at least a day or two a week until they are 22. If you cannot do that, review the way you act that induces pregnancy within you or the one who is with you.

Whatever you do, you will be held responsible for it. If you do not agree, look at others and see why you are blind to what you can be but see their lives as easy. If you cannot advise another in the ethical structure of being a parent now, you are not one. If you say you are but cannot put it into words, you are not trying hard to be the best parent you can be.

Words precede the works of so many on Earth that we expect and sometimes require that you talk about whatever you want first. If you are a quiet one, you can go inside and decide--otherwise, go to the world and proclaim what you want in this life and make it happen. You will thrive.

If the world can help you do what you want, it will generally supply you with the means to be. But if you want something that runs counter to the world and what others need from you to exist, you will receive nothing. You can always count on God to agree to anything that will help thee!

Whatever you believe and do and conceive is you.

If your mind is full of advice from others, when do you decide who you will be? We would never ask you to try to be Maya, too, but you are and will be whoever you conceive you to be. You are Maya? You will be a Maya.

If you conceive the birth of you in the flesh of a tribe living in Guatemala at this time, you might not find it possible to be Maya now, but you might visit them and see what you believe is the life you miss. You will be delighted to return home. You miss nothing if you have never been there in the first place. But if you yearn to return to a spot on Earth, you lived there once. Go to Paris or Rome and see what it is you are attracted to see. We watched the artist in Ruth Lee travel to Paris and return three times in three days to Montmartre where she bought an artist's rendition of the scene. What do you think that says about Ruth Lee?

You will find that you are not the only Maya this time who is not living in Mexico or Guatemala, but you will find that there are many others who are around who are also tribal and seem to appeal to you now as well as the Maya at times. What do you make of that? You are partial to others who are a lot like you or you are not a Maya and have been a friend to one in the past who taught you to do what you do. If you doubt that is true, try to think of a club on Earth that you love and would want to join, but they do not admit you. What do you do? Do you pine or try to live like them all the time? That is what you will do when you find out that some will never be Maya but you may be one.

You are not to pine or whine for a time when you had more power. You have power now. You are who defines what you do and whining wears at the ears and turns off everyone. You cannot be a whiner and finish on time.

The Word of The Maya

If you are tired of working with others and believe you can succeed by working as a scribe and becoming a woman of personality and worth, try to imitate The Scribe and become alive to all others. She is unable to take back much from all this work because the cash is always put back into other work. So there you have nothing to sit on and brood upon and wish to do more within the present economy, but you might believe that others do better. That is the way of the ignorant and the envious today. You do not have more or less than you have the need to produce or you would work harder. If you do work hard, all things will come through for you. Do not give it away. If you do, how much money do you require to be God for a day?

Most people refuse to believe that today is all there is. What day do you see today to be? What are you doing for you? Are you living in the past and proud to confuse you with myths? When you live in the day after today—or tomorrow, you produce anxiety and a degree of disbelief in what you can be. But you will never be too far wrong if your way of dealing with others is to follow the path you are on today and live for the best. If you try to be crooked and deny another the path, it will take you away from the straightway that leads to You.

If you do something you honestly do not believe is wrong, what happens to you? You are shown the proper way if wrong. If you are told to do something and refuse to do whatever it is they all think you should do, you will lose in some significant way--but it may still be best for you.

Earth is not a project you do, but a way to see what you can do. If you cannot complete the work of being you, what else is more important than you?

Ruth Lee, Scribe

Look at Earth!

What being in the Earth seems to be looking back at you? You! You are a part of the Earth, too. The chemicals and trace minerals within you are not of the soul and will not prepare you to fly from Earth when this sojourn is over, so what do you say about Earth now and what it does to you?

If you have no explanation for it, do you respect what the elders around you say and do? You know you do. You watch to see what adults do when you are small. Today adults are very short and their children quite tall. Is that why the children so often look down on adults now and frown at their elders? You do, too, if you are a fool.

If you want to know more, go to those who went before you. If you want to ignore what they do, ask them first what they did that did not work and do whatever you intend to do then. Only a fool would ignore what worked for others in the past.

If you refuse to accept that you may not be an expert yet, you can expect many more to help you and provide information and certain assistance to you so you will suffer no pain. But if you never let on you need help, who will want to be of assistance to you? You. You always have You to ask what to do, but you have to establish the path or you will get lost trying to find the way back.

When you hack out a path that grows back, the dense underbrush is even denser than it was. Look back and review that sentence and see what it says about you and what you do. Are you able to make a similar contrast in what you spiritually seek within you as you read?

The Word of The Maya

Let us laugh!

You are who you are and we are Maya who are not like you. What do you think we look like? We want you to contract to write up a paragraph and follow it up with a picture of you dressed to be a Maya who will pass into the next avenue.

Place a picture frame on this page to surround your drawing.

• **A Portrait of Me Being Maya** •

The Word of The Maya

The worlds of The Maya are not easily drawn by one who is not able to see into destiny, but you are. Draw and write and work all night. A dream will give you all you need to stay alive and be.

If you can draw a Maya as you imagine in a tribe and doing what you believe, it is fantasy. To be Maya is a belief and not a fantasy. Beliefs are inside and fantasies come to be and are conceived through the intervention of the mind. Beliefs are at a level beyond time.

You are now in time? You are and will be as long as you reside on Earth and feel that you are a member of this race. If you drop out and live as animals should, you might find that you are able to tell the moon and the sky what to do, and they will stay there all the time. But if you are Maya, you learn to tell the world what time is by looking at the sky.

You are the sky. You are the world. You wonder why, buy know it is, and the belief is so deep within you that you cannot find words to explain it. You will have to subside or rise with each tide and wonder why.

What takes time?
you

You take time and misuse it all the time in order to wonder why you must be here at this time. Why do you do that? If you can accept that you are as you are and will be human and do what you do for this time, will you succeed beyond the wildest beliefs of others who are human, too? Why? You accept that everything as unique. There is no measure you can use to discover you or the process of others who are doing what they are here to do. You are all too unique to judge what each other must be, but inside you, all know what you alone must be and do before you can all go home.

Home is Earth as long as you sojourn and work along in this work, but it will expand to combine again into the harmonics of others who are also living on Earth and expand to join the band of philharmonics that create the band that leaves Earth and joins others from other Earths and works to achieve the universal verse.

Poetry comes from beyond the Earth. Words can be rhymed by the mind, but they never suit the occasion as well as those that seem to overwhelm the personality at birth and at times when they realign with the Earth. You are not a poet? You were one at birth. What did you do to the poet within you? You never wrote. If you never do anything ever, do you atrophy or grow within you? What do you think?

Write a poem about the day you left school and never again took up the tool that lets you pretend to be you. Write with pen or pencil now and produce a poem that will serve as a reminder of what you must do in this life.

LIVE is the title and you will write:

When Julie Powell writes and you read, are you working earnestly? You will now proceed to read what you have written and not judge The Scribe, Julie Powell, or others for what they write. Why? You are to become a scribe inside and write every day of your life. If you do, then we will permit you to criticize the writing of others, too.

The Scribe is permitted to teach you writing because she is not letting it pile up for centuries and not working to become yet a better writer. Are you? The Scribe is not paid handsomely to write this way, but The Maya will take her away at the end of time. Is that not the way of life?

What do you want to be when you write? Is it an ego pursuit that you think will achieve money or fame--ego gratification if you are able to say you write? What do you want to achieve? Writing the way you are taught on Earth today is not the way, but it helps to begin that way. Why? You are human and need to be human or the God of All would not have let you choose to be human.

If you choose to do what God does not allow anyone else to do, will you be chastised? You do not succeed. If no one is allowed to kill others and continue to breathe and live successfully, why would you believe you could be the one to succeed over everyone? You would have a mind that misleads you through time. If your mind is telling you lies all the time, you will not know what to do when the end of time comes to you, but we can still be there to help you. Why? We are here to help people escape Earth and move to the next line.

Ruth Lee, Scribe

Respectfully submitted by Ruth Lee, Scribe
Witnessed by Julie Powell

Chapter Eleven

THE MAYA WORK FOR YOU

Whatever you are doing now, stop!
What did you do?

Are you confused? Are you unable to do what you are asked to do? Most people who are confused are that way because they refuse to compute. Why? Who knows, but they do. The work of others may be so inferior or superior that some will not let it come through, but most are too lazy to want to work on You and what YOU sends you to do.

When will you work?
What will you do?

Are you a shaman waiting to work on you? Are you sitting and working at a page or two a day, trying to write a novel about you? Are you willing to work hard for you or sitting and reading in order to avoid hard work?

Ruth Lee, Scribe

Writing is the spiritual outlet of many who are trying to fly high. Are you the scribe and author of books that others frequently ask to look at and understand? What if you are? We are not admirers of The Scribe and others because they write and work for hours. We are here to work through The Scribe as well as all others who are fit to work in this work. What about you? If you are unfit to work and do only what is placed in front of you, what do you expect The Maya to teach you?

When you drive your own life into the middle of the road and refuse to let others pass by, what are you doing? You are stagnating, like many others. All of you clog the road of life now, trying to stop the tide. Why? If you cannot climb aboard the train and enter the first car and find a seat, where do you stand then? You may remain in the first car and clog the train so others will have to ignore you and push you aside or be unable to move further than you. What do you do usually?

Think of all the things you can be and see what comes through.

What did you see?

Are you now living in that dream? When you arrive safely on time, are you happy or relaxed or just not aware that you passed another test on time?

When time comes for you, will you be able to pass it, too? Think of it as a class. You are in the work of two or three others who are unique and part of you, and you all have to combine at some time and intertwine and unite and be You. If you doubt that is possible, look at the work of Ruth and see what you can be, too. She is not able to write about herself or you or the others who walk into her life, but we do.

Ruth Lee is a personality who has a lot of life inside her one life this time, but not half as much as the three beings who make up the Ruth of Ruth Lee. You may wonder why Ruth Lee is in the tribe, but we believe she has always written as a scribe and will die a scribe and be retrieved in other lives to scribe, but what about you? What do you believe is true?

When you dance and prance and play around, do you feel the breath as though you were having an asthma attack? If so, you will end the being that is you and continue into the next you or the next you until you are ready to be You.

What makes you upset?

Are you afraid to discuss death? Are you so alive that you cannot imagine when you die? What do you do now that is so marvelous to others that you cannot go? Why should you be alive and let the rest die?

What about you cannot pass the test? A series of lines that made you either sublime or filled you with unrest. What do you think about the test and the way you intend to pass along with the rest? Are you aware that time is the only element that all on Earth must pass? Are you aware that you pass time all the way along the line? What do you do now to clear you and your line? Are you so clogged that only God knows you?

Where is the line to the inner being, the spine, and the mind that makes you seem sublime? Where are you? Are you able to comprehend even one line at this time? Which line ends your peace of mind?

Write out what is now stopping you from reading as fast you usually do.

Ruth Lee, Scribe

_____
_____
_____
_____
_____
_____
_____
_____
_____
_____
_____
_____
_____
_____
_____

Do scenes of childhood flash in your mind from time to time? What color do you paint that time? Are you bright and shiny in those days of your youth and want them to remain within you, or do you work up a design that includes grime, pain, and misuse in order to say that you could not be you because of the parents who gave you life in order to live for you? What excuse is useful when you are a success and happy to be you?

Whatever you do, do it for you and the people who surround you. Why care about others who are not there for you? You are not there for them either, but if all of you work together to grow further than each of you could grow if you worked only on you, you will all fly together into the blue and be able to do more and more for YOU. We promise.

The Word of The Maya

You have it all now, so get together!

Chapter Twelve

MAYA WORK WITHIN THE VEIL

When you enter the room of your own home and find it disturbed, is your mind able to find home? Not there. It goes to another place and time and sits until it can find the way to the spot where it is. You live in a veil all this time and may wonder why you live in a house or an apartment or a hut or whatever, but you live. You design the outer accouterments all this time, but you live as is.

You will be. You will see, but you will give up the first layer of love inside you if you live inside another's house only to live. If you want to feel yourself, you need to be you. If you cannot, then leave the environs and move inside and decide why. If you are unable to live in the heart of your own mind, are you totally bereft of fame and fortune and merely want what others have?

You must love you. If you cannot love you and what you produce, your mind is totally confused about you, and you are not helping you. If unable to feel good, you are not doing the work of you. We would work today on finding you, but you have to veil the truth now.

What do you do to examine a new belief? First, you decide that it is not true. You do! You do what you always do. If the new belief makes a lot of sense to you, maybe you will believe it or maybe you will perceive it, but you have to live it before it can be you. Why? You are in the veil.

Are you in a veil of tears and fear all who are around you? What do you do now?

Are you full of interest in others who are not like you and would you love to be one of them in order to explain who you are to you? You might become an anthropologist once or in each life if so. If not, you would study you. The way to study you is to just do it. If you study anyone other than you, you produce static within you that causes feuds with anyone with sense who does not want you to study them instead of working on you.

When you study psychology and view you, are you hurting you? Not if you look with love at what you do. If you cannot do that, you might find someone to help you, but it will not work for you if you do not work on you, too. Many of you never do.

What to do?
Enter your own home and sit there

If your home is new and you feel that it is a strange venue, will you feel as good as if you were in a place where you are more accustomed than this? Probably for an hour or two, then you will move You into this home with you. It is a fact that you can accomplish more in a second or two than in a lifetime if you decide to move, but most do, see, and believe that they do not need to move. We do. Enter your own life. End the tyranny of blaming others for what you do to you. That is all you need to do to be you.

If you think others make demands upon you, think about what you do to them. What do you talk about with them? Are you always poking at them and demanding things from them or their ways and means, and whoever is wrong is berated? If so, you are being paid back for sending out a feud to others and not taking care of you.

Work is doing for you. You do the world a favor when you take care of you. What work should you do? Stop and listen and work to do everything you do as perfectly as you can, then do it even better. You will stretch your mind, your soul will do fine, and the life you live will improve.

What do you need to stay in your own time? A mind. When your mind needs dusting off and trotted out to see what it missed, you are totally out of it, or drank or ingested a drug that did it to you. What do you do to you to forget? You have to forget? You do if you want to commit to being a new person. If you forget who you are and fully get over it, you will not be confused later when others try to make you go to a home where you would not like to die. You are who will be there at the end, so be sure you prepare your own bed.

When you move and do something new, are you being you or doing something to you that makes you someone new? Think over that line and decide for yourself this time.

We are not here to do all the work for you to ascend at the end, but you are beginning to believe we should do it for you. Why? You think The Maya are wise enough so you do not have to use time as well as we do. That is a lie! You have to learn how to tell you what time is and why you live this way before you can give up this breath and move onto the next time or episode within your mind.

You live many lives within one time?
You do now!

Why are you so sure that this life is real and all others do not exist? What do you do to exist within this you? What do you think about others who are unable to trust you? Are you trustworthy and they are dishonest? Honestly, are you who caused them not to love you? What do you do to others?

When you go within the veil of You to do whatever you came to do, will you do it for You or for you? What do you think will happen to this you? What did it mean to you to see the veil torn in half from top to bottom by the Lord of All when the temple fell? Did you laugh then? No, because you saw the power of God in all. You are like that. You can move the power of God through you that rends you in two if you want to do it over in twos. If you wanted to design a new lifeline, you would split you in half, but that is not exactly how you do that to you.

What to do to make sure you are who you are? Be you and laugh at anyone who is unwilling to see you in this way. If you do not believe in you, you get upset if another teases you. That is true! Why would you say it is not? You know you do not believe in you, but you do not think that anyone else can see that, too. We do and so do the wise among you. Believe in you, then all of us will see that you are tough and able to follow the path all the way through the veil to the top of YOU and not get lost.

The Word of The Maya

What if you try to tease someone else into believing in us? We know if you do that, and we do not appreciate the joke. We do not like the idea of telling others not to smoke, either, but the ether of the world is such that we need to say it for thee.

Do not smoke!

If you drink a lot of things that make you feel strange and weird, you are doing that to you. If you drive into a tree you hurt the universe by killing someone who is then being a tree, but you may not feel it really counts because you do not see the being in the tree. What do you see?

What if the veil over you is so deep and detailed that you cannot feel it? What do you believe? You see? You are not able to see. You have not one care that makes you beware of living in the deep despair of this life and wanting more. You have no chores. You can be lazy and seem to be obviously too jealous of others to be any more good to the class, but we can teach you to behave as you believe. We will torture you with the memory of what you can be.

When do you feel betrayed? Never? Good. You are not doing that to you in any way today. If you are anxious over and over again, you betray you over and over again.

If your mind is full of time, yet it is never a good time for you to gain, what does it say? You are not helping you to live within for you, but you think someone else is. You are not observing what others give. If you strive always to live as is and never give, what does it do for you? You will feel that it is you who gives too much to others, and not like the feeling. If you are upset and nervous with others, you are denying that it is you and not them who upsets you within.

If your mind is upset and nervous, are you responsible? What do you need to know before you grow? What is on your mind? What does it mean to understand time?

We will help you grow and do more in time, but you have to know how to end the tyranny of the mind. If you go into the outer regions of soul and Spirit says it is time to move on, you go. But if you are tired and do not respond, the soul will send you another being to help you--an emissary from across the bridge of time. You will know and go, but someone had to be sent to help you, and that means you are slow.

If you are able to grasp instantly what this class is about, and slow down long enough to grasp more and more of the information that the class is doing without being bored, you are going to arrive at each assignment on time and be able to do whatever you have to do. You will also learn something new. If you do not go inside the mind enough, or grow beyond this time on Earth, you do not want to know and try to slow you and others with talk about money and stuff. You could be left at the end of this time by doing it over and over and slowly learning that you do not know enough. Why take so long to discover that? Why not do it all together and laugh?

What do you do when you see all the way through to YOU? You let go. You does not stop you and you from joining into a third personality who is able to go beyond you to know You are capable of doing it all. If you know now exactly what we said in that line, you are ahead of time but will have to go back and forth until others catch up with you. Why not wait here and sit within you and know that the others will join you?

We want you to understand that some move faster than others because they choose a better path. Yes, and you know that one path provides more of pain or sorrow and joy or laughter than others, but you chose the path. Do not linger over the same old lessons so you do not have to work. Work on the path you chose and never do it over again. Get going today on taking over the old way and doing it a better way. We need you.

If you are called to work on the work of God of All, how do you answer? You work. You do the work first and say later that you answered the call. If you do it the other way, you might not be able to do anything. You have to see what it is before you can conceive of the way to be.

The work of being is conceiving that you do believe and you do whatever you see. Truly the way to work and do what you see is to believe, but many of you are not willing to prepare to work on you. We are ready, but are you?

What to do to prepare you? You will do it because it will never be done for you. When you are ready, please review the first three chapters of this book, then do it over and over until you feel you are able to do whatever you do over and over without making mistakes as you do it. We will answer no questions from you about YOU? You have none. Your mind may decide to whine and ask a lot of questions to stall you in this time, but not YOU. YOU knows You well enough to give only what you need to do, so never question God of All about what you have to do. You already know.

You will find that the time to go and mend the veil is when you are over and done with the work of this Earth. Are you done? Then you can mend the work you do, too. We will help you go back and forth with it to discover what is not done well enough by you to help you. If the motion of going beyond you is too much for you, sit and reveal that you believe you are far enough along with the work you came to do. You are not, but the mind often says you understand time when you do not. We do, but we can see most are not willing to accept what we do. You will, but not until you see that no one on Earth is free of time and can teach you about it now.

When The Maya free themselves of those who disbelieve in what they see, they talk like you talk and see what you see; however, they believe and see and become. You do not. You look up at a star and stalk it with a scope all night as if that one being is all there is. Why not look at the entire scope and wonder about who the stars are now?

What you see is a personality? You are. What kind of being creates you, or a tree, or doing work on a car? You and the others who compose this star. You are all seen by those in outer space as a single being, but you are you. You now seek them? You have no need to be one of them, but you are. You are who you are, but some of you beam to others on other stars. What? Yes, you can. You can be strong and bright and able to light the sky with your own light. We want you to do that tonight.

If you think you always have to wait until night to live and divide the day into two segments, you do not live during the day; but sleep is not what we are all about. We dream and work at the inner seam of this life with you inside trying to open to the brighter side. We can work now, but you must dream.

If you cannot sleep, you cannot be. If you never sleep, the dream will never be complete. Your mind will collapse and your lungs will not be able to breathe as fast as they did before. You need rest. The body repairs itself when you sleep, but you also renew the inner being, too.

The Word of The Maya

You are not able to veil your illusions now? You do. You never believe anything you cannot see? We see you and believe in you, but since you cannot beam us into your own view, you do not see us and believe that we know all about you. Try now to do that for you--beam in the light of The Maya within You.

Work is being done today to help you always, but do you want to move inside of you and do whatever you came to do for You? What does that mean to you? If you remain a fool, you will read and not listen to anyone, but you continue to read. If you are wise, you have completed all the exercises and have a full grasp of time now. What kind of man or woman says he or she is wise yet cannot do the work required inside? A fool.

You will be able to do more and more within You, but will it do much for you personally during this life or two? You are what you do. If you cannot connect within You and be you, can You help you become a star? No, but you are. You shine regardless of where you are, but some of you veil your life in water so much that you never share a thing of what you are with others.

Cry!

See? You cannot cry when you are wise. Only the wise would read deeply into this message now, so we are able to confer upon you that title and not feel foolish in any way doing it.

If you can read faster than anyone else on Earth, what does it mean? Are you reading or just rehearsing the lines for another verse? What do the lines mean? Are you able to comprehend at all times what they are saying and doing today and what they will produce within you? You see now? Not if you cannot read what you see. If you can see and believe a lot of things, your mind is open at all times and may even be too wide for you to be certain of what you believe. Be you! Open when you have to believe in you and close when others try to shove you into the opening of wherever they are going.

Why?

You may not be moving as slowly as they and may not be able to stop the delay in time to go beyond this work and do what you came to do for You. Be sure you know why you tag along with others over time, and once you do know, be sure they are headed down the same path as you are or you will be lost before the second bend in the road. We know what to do, but do you?

Your work on time is about to end. If you cannot comprehend it, please do over any exercise that helps your mind bend. If you cannot do anything over and change what you do then, you are as far as you can go. If you can change so many things you did before, and now know so much more about you than you ever did before, you are ready to end this listener's mode and go within. We want you to do that now.

Go inside your mind and pretend...

Go inside your mind and work behind this scene to end this time. Pretend that you are flying to the next mode of love and can fly high above all others standing in line now. Look down the road and see why they are waiting or working on something that cannot be seen.

Look in--between the lines. Reread all the things that Ruth Lee brings you. Go back and read what you never saw and see if it rhymes more or less than it did before. If you can do this, you will grow more and more each time you refine the lines. If the lines all appear to be exactly as before, you cannot learn more.

You determine why you exist and why you co-exist with others? You are here to learn lessons on the way to live, but time is the coordinating factor between you and others. If you never keep appointments with others, you have no friends. If you are constantly late or too early to arrive on time with friends, you have not met the one who is able to bend into the same line as you all the time and those friendships will end.

Whatever you do, study you. Work for the real world to follow you and not be a party to anyone who is destroying the truth about you. You permit it? You are doing you in with it then. You are who must assure the world that you fit in, but do it in a way that does not threaten others who pray. You can play and admit many things to your elders that would not be fit for the ears or others, but you cannot admit to torturing others and ever fit in. You will be punished for it.

What?

You heard the three rules when you came to Earth:

1. You must learn to tolerate all others and be fit.

2. You must work on you all the days of your life until you are through with it.

3. Harm no living being. It will be held against you if you do.

Ruth Lee, Scribe

These three beliefs make a better woman and man than one without an ethical structure in place today. Use the rules. You can confuse your mind with whatever religious belief you find sublime.

You will find that time is not of the essence in everyone. You think it is? You now find the way to decide what is truth today. We congratulate you!

Respectfully submitted by
The Scribe
August 18, 1997

Chapter Thirteen

MAYA WORK WITHIN YOUR WORK

The race is over! You are either a winner or a loser based on the standards of everyone around you now, but you are who you are. Either you are able to be you or you have lost the essence of what you could and would have been if you had allowed you to be you now. You are who damages you when you let others get all the way through to You, then do what you do not want to do. You are who must call upon You and ask for the right to participate in your own life, but do it after we are done with this work.

You work and you talk and you walk or whatever to get around the world or you cannot feel how much freedom is around you now. You cannot feel like you if you never walk out of your room and visit others who are a lot like you or not one iota like you. Why? You are tested by others.

If you want to work like a Maya now, do not don work that they do today and say it is your work, but put on the work of the Lord of the Maya and You and others, then do what you know must be done to free you. No religion on Earth is like you, but you can adopt one or two. More than one religious point of view would cause you to stop seeing you as you are and easy for you to be damaged beyond what You could do for you now. But to do more and more thought in one line of religious education now is not upsetting to most who are on Earth--but it bothers you a lot.

If you think you alone are lonely or blue or sad or upset about what goes on around you, you upset you. If you struggle and work to accrue a living and others rob you, you can be upset yet it will help you. What kind of life did you produce for you? Are you upsetting you or being upset by others who refuse to let you work for you?

When you drive a car or a vehicle now, you all obey the rules. If you do not, someone is hurt and penalties given to all fools. However, you may not think those same penalties apply to everything you do within the other aspects of your lives, too. Do you speed? You want to move faster than is legal in the eyes of authorities in place. You want to pass on the inside? You want to take the easiest route and beat out those beside you, but you may not live to see the day because you drove forward in a very rash way.

What if you break down along the way? Will anyone else stop and help you? It is obvious; someone will come along and help you. If you doubt it, stop and look, see how many come up to you and ask if you need help. If you receive no help today, ask yourself, when was the last time I stopped to help anyone else? You see? Perhaps not, but you will find out that points are accrued over the life you prove to be you. If you do not see anyone else but you, your misery is all within you.

The Word of The Maya

We want you to decide right now to work for you in an unfamiliar way so you can see that greed and pride are not always visible. If you watch another tribe work and go inside the lines of their communication and beat a drum, you can find a way to talk to them then, yet not be included in what they think or believe in any way.

You cannot be you?

If you adopt the beliefs of others, you are trying to be someone you are not. If you do that now, you will have nothing left at the end of the day.

Believe in you

What about that line sounds old and trite and not wise? You. You are who still does not see the beauty of you if you cannot see that line is perfectly true and will not be undone no matter what kind of editor you think you may be.

You will see that many pretend to be writers and such and do nothing at all but collect much, then rewrite it over and over again until it sounds better to them--but what about the original writers?

Many Maya study the skies at this time, but none know much about it. Why? The Maya proceeded to believe in the beauty of the scribe and let the scribe write whatever he believed. The scribe was never criticized, never told what to say--except by someone else who could write. You see? Writers are never criticized unless you write, too. You have to write to be able to work inside lines of the Bible and Koran and books of wisdom from other lands. You cannot just read it.

You have to be able to decide what is right, not The Scribe, but some of you are lazy and will accept what is written verbatim instead of really studying the book. We want you to realize soon that you have to be you and that you have many who are always there to stand at your side and work with you. The Maya are just one of the tribes now alive willing to step up the work they do to include you. Are you willing to be Maya, too?

What tribe?
What Maya wants you?
You

You are the tribe and the tribe is You, but you think only of the many who live on Earth, who are primitive and unable to do what each of you do as a tribe when all people around you live in tribes.

Corporate people never look at the crowds of people who flock around artists and such, but we do. Artists disdainfully stay as far from the market as they can until they need funds, but we know that you see them travel and eat and have fun. What do you know about the tribe you go around with now? Are you the leader? Are you a scribe and write to everyone in your family all the time to keep them posted about what is going on now? Are you the clown who eliminates the static when others become too close to happily fit in one room? Are you the deserter who is unwilling to admit that you do have a family and have to commit? Which role best describes you?

The clown is the best one to be if you have a family that is divergent and low in the economy. You know you fit. You never get hysterical or nervous, but you are fit. You go out knowing what bothers others and you diffuse the wrath of the elders and do whatever you see as fit. The clown knows more than the most serious psychologist can fit in a book about what it takes to raise a family today. Ask one now!

What did you do? Are you able to rise from a book and do what you are asked to do immediately? Most of you do not think that fast, but some will not follow through, no matter what the class. Why read? Why study? Why write? To know you.

You can pass anybody. Know that and get inside the work you do for You and work on you. Do it now and fly to the end of Earth and do your own life over and over until you know what you do and why it is you.

Is there anything else you can do? When you are given such a huge assignment, what do you normally do? For now, sit and smile. Look inside you. Go back and slowly reread that last paragraph back to you.

What are you doing now? Are you pursuing You? If you are, please continue. If you are not, sit.

When you return to work with The Maya, and the calendar is ticking and sticking in your mouth and you are worried about the day of the month, sit. If you can now just sit and smile and follow all the way through to being the clown, please be one now.

What did you do? Are you hysterical over being you? Why not admit that you are foolish enough to take you very seriously all day through? If you refuse to see how much you believe about You that is not smart or easy to believe, you admit nothing. Why not believe in You now?

Ruth Lee, Scribe

When you can be You, and smile all the way through to the clown you are, work on it. Work on you now.

What time do you have? You have time to be and time to see that your work is all meant to make you be you. If you do not see that now, no amount of work with The Maya will help you go beyond this work now.

Respectfully submitted,
Ruth Lee, Scribe, August 20, 1997

Chapter Fourteen

MAYA WRITING WITH WHAT YOU HAVE IN MIND

You have nothing to do? Not true, you are always doing something, and if you believe otherwise, you are not wise. If you see immediately that you can be anything you wish to be and are willing to compromise to achieve it, you will be. But if you cannot scheme and dream and visualize, what becomes of your life?

Realize that you are and will be whatever you are doing now, and you will continue to be exactly as you are until you change by some appreciable degree. If you cannot fully appreciate that you are a work of art and doing what you want to do, change you until you can see through to the being who is You, then ask for directions. That is smart, but you are old enough to be aware by now that you are and can be whatever you do and see--not what you dream, unless you work hard.

If every one of us and you were to build a temple to God of All and watch it go up, who do you think would be at the top? You? If you believe that, you have an ego that is very defeatable. If you think you deserve to work hard and you do it all day long, you might find a part of the temple that is yours to do over and over again, but would you lead? Would you be able to do more and more with others who also achieve what you believe? Are you able to see that the leader is a follower who is able to do the work and follow, then jump in and lead the group to the top?

Are you aware of what you do today that makes you the way you are? What about You is confusing to you? What do you do that makes you wish you were bigger than others? Nothing, but the ego of you will produce an enzyme within you that makes you feel larger than you are. What? Yes, the body produces many excuses for you to believe that you can achieve without being yourself or doing the work of others who would elect you to lead them to do more, but all of you on Earth are not able to produce a lot without direction and guidance from the planes above Earth. Why? You are only partially realized.

You feel partial? Then you cannot feel. You sense that you have a lot of decay in your body now? No, but there is constant rebuilding going on now. What does it do to you? You are constantly being renewed by the body of you--a kind of locomotive work of art that changes the part you play every day or so.

You will find that if you can be kind to the work and let it alone that it works, but if you are inclined to meddle with it all day, the body begins to do less and less and never plays. Are you dismayed that the body is not yours at all? You must have realized that the body is used only for a 'day' and then given away.

The Word of The Maya

You will find that Earth is a kind of laboratory in which you all decided to live. You all have time to flap your wings or be less kind, but you will find that by the end of a 'day', or a life in your mind, you will have lived in each kind of being you see and admire and wish to be; but will you be anyone at all? You are. You cannot be what you are? You have now. You achieve now. You are the work of art you breathe now!

What does it take to humiliate the mind? Not much at times, yet at other times the mind will refrain from listening to the brain. You have been through it all. You have to decide now what it is you do in the fall that comes back in the spring, if you do remember to think.

Think? What do you think? What makes you drink? What makes you sit somewhere and think of things you can be and yet not try to achieve even a small bit of the dream? You! You stop you and blame others for not helping you.

Who supports you? Are you taken to court? Are you really who is the one they caught? Are you really who is stopped? You did it all and watched from the wings the act you committed to You and the human being of you, but YOU is there watching you get on with things.

You have to do more? You are who decided to quit and not do it. If you want to move, do it, but do not say that it is not the way you would have lived if someone else had given you more. You do all things and you think about whatever brings you pain or sorrow or relief. What do you bring to YOU when you think about you?

If you are afraid of others, do you shrink? You do. You must shrink from evil or you will walk into the room of others who do not like you and be taken from You. You do not notice that happen? Do you ever walk into a room of people who are not able to love or be loved by others and think they will admire you? What kind of people do you think are evil?

When you are unable to love you and do for you what you should do for anyone who is like you, what do you believe another should achieve and give to you? That is evil of you! You were sure you deserved what someone else did and gave to you? If you think about it now, as a child you were exposed to evil all the time and never submitted until now to the belief that somehow the work you do should be rewarded by others and that you should not have to do anything for it. Why would an adult expect that? The child was never told any better.

You cannot suddenly learn to work for a living if you never had to do anything before you left your mother or father and had to make a living. You will expect others to give it to you and smile.

What a life! You were surprised? What do you expect others to do for you? Write a list now of all that you take for granted and expect others to do for you today.

_____
_____
_____
_____
_____
_____
_____
_____
_____
_____

_____
_____
_____
_____

Was there enough room to list everything? You have taken much, but now you are an adult and expected to give to the child. What do you intend to do? Go back over the list and eliminate all the things you can do for yourself.

Did you erase or did you place them in a different line and think about each one? Did you strike out a line and rewrite it again over time? How do you eliminate what is not good for you to do?

When you erase a line, it eliminates that time, but that time is not inside you. You will do fine, but if you eliminate time, you feel blue from time to time and may whine about others who are not with you now. Do not refuse to erase you, but be sure you can stand the test of time when others will not be with you because you ended that relationship, too.

When you draw a line here, you think of time, but maybe never did before now. You are going to see whatever you will not be, but it will still stay there and be legible over time and may remind you over and over again about what you have done with this thing you want to remove from your mind. Why not erase it now? You can, but the line is easier now.

Smile if you never erased anything!

You have to admire the child within you. If you have a child so big within you now that you feel you deserve everything, think of you as the biggest ego in your crew. The ego represents the child still working within you. Are you ready to be adult, too?

What you do in the mind affects you all the time, so we have made a long lesson today to show the way to go inside you and bless the way you will work today. Think of you.

What? You did not stop? You will now stop and sit and dream and think of YOU. When you are through dreaming and being you, what do you do?

Can you now read and be content with doing a lesson that will be a blessing to you one day? No, you are working today on you. Your work is not with Ruth Lee, but with You and YOU. You have to be able to see that you are supported regardless of what you do, so believe in You and that the YOU of all there is within you will protect you, and God of All will take up the crew who are prepared to rise with you when the time of this life is through.

Believe in you?
What else can you do?

You are the only one now who is aware of what you need or do, so what do you think will happen when you no longer have to breathe? Do you think you will simply disappear into a room of evil or good and everything will be done for you? What in life prepared you for the other side? You. We will, too, but you have spiritual guides who live all this life with you and are able to steer you from one task or ruse to another. What do you choose to do?

If you say you are spiritually guided, but it does not work out as you were told, do you claim it failed because a Guide who asked you to do it betrayed you? If so, you are a child and will be scolded for not following the work of the elder who told you not to do what someone else told you to do. You are you and able to sit in the pool of this life and be bathed and pampered with love and advice, but you still have to grow up and admit that you did it. You are who can ask for advice and live it, but you must be sure you asked the right guide.

What? You have more than one limit? You are not able to just sit and ask anyone how to live it? You are now aware that there are several people within you, and you are several egoistic states at times, too, and you do want to do what adults do, too. We whine? No, you do. You have egos and minds and times you do not want to do, so you submit to any amount of pressure and desire from others to stay as you are. You can, but you lose what this you could do, too.

Why not change every day or so into another feature of you? You know--be a nose. We jest. You must laugh at you and know that you can do some things well and other things not without a lot of mess. We know you. You have to see that we are talking about you being you in a time when it is not as sublime as usual, but Earth is a place to maintain a state of grace, too. You will find some do while some feud all the time. What do you do?

Now, let us return with a smile to see you changing you and trying to be another creature, too. You can do it. You can decide to change from a man into a woman and back again, but others will not admire that in you. Why? You refuse to align at the base of the spine and accept what God has assigned you to do this time. As a result, you are always in a state of flux and have very little luck. You can now change from a man into a woman and never have another love of the same kind that you came to Earth to prepare to seek, and you still whine.

What creates a whine? A strained muscle and a strong mind resisting needed rest.

If the mind is inclined to sit and wonder why, what do you do all the time? You whine. You are still not fit? You did it. You cannot be fit and whine about it. One does not fit into the other unless you let the fit body relax so much that it now does not fit into the clothes you buy. Why? You did it. Take credit for the decision or change it.

You will find that talking about weight and body all the time is a way of doing nothing about it. You can talk and others become aware that you are not sure what it is you did, but they tire of it. You will find no one who is busy cares about the body as much as the body.

If you ignore the body, and ignore the armor that protects you from others, you will in time be defeated by it. But if the body and your ego mind are able to protect you and keep you from those around you who propose to take over your work, you will be fine. You can see what comes through the line.

What line?
Are you being attacked?

You are being attacked all the time, but notice only if one line of defense is stronger or weaker then. You are able to pick up many things that others pretend to think all the time, but will they ever do them? You are not doing one millionth of the billions of things you will think about during this life, so why would any one else do what you think they will do? You watch to see what they do.

You are not dumb, nor are you Number One. You are here to do more and more, and you will be taught by a score of elders before you are through with this world, but will you do anything?

When you have done the work of one, do you feel more? You do. You have nothing at all now that cannot work within you, but what is not working must be stopped and propped by the door. You will take it outside later and deposit it where others can pick it up or use what you did not need for you-- like putting out the garbage.

You will do whatever you do, and then stew if you are afraid of others who are just like you. If you believe you are superior to others, you do little. You do not believe you have to work. But if you have a little bit of sense within you, you notice others working to get to the top of this heap and working in a group at least once to do something significant and good. What do you think you will do?

Are you ready to submit to an adult task and work within you to do what You and the other *yous* within you believe will help you?

Are you truly able to follow up on what you think of you? What did you do in the past?

Think now of all the mean people who are always working within you trying to decide what you should do.

What did you do just now?

Are you capable of thinking of meanness in this lesson about you? What did you really do? Are you so suspicious of others that you never do anything with anyone other than you? You are then a whiner over time. You will never do much but believe that others did it to you.

Ruth Lee, Scribe

What do whiners do?

Usually they end up drinking or using the work of others. We know. We watch the planet grow from one vineyard to millions who want to have bottles at their elbow. What do you hide? Where are the adults inside your mind?

What does a child know that the adult must be well educated to know? YOU. You have found over time the means to hide and not know YOU all the time, but a child does know all that is and will be and gives up when adults are unwilling to help the child know and grow.

You are a child now? You need to know that if God has blessed you with a strong gift you need not let anyone else know now, but once you are able to use it, you must practice and make it appear within you all day, too. Why? You are aware now that you are able to do what you know. No adult is needed if that is the reason you came to earth now. You are here to show adults that a child can know God.

When you decide that you have open eyes, yet others are closed to the light of God and you are not, what do you do? You work on being you. If you are filled with anger or whatever, or proud of you now, you will lose what you are and only God will know how much you have to be proud about now. If you enjoy being you, who can make you feel upset? You is the only one who really gets to you, so do what you are and will be and let the rest know you are happy to be you now. We are.

When working within the mind all the time, the idea that you cannot be Maya appears. Why? You see a tribe and think that The Maya are dead, and though you feel inside that you can fly and do whatever you want before you die, how can

The Word of The Maya

they be inside me? Right? No, but it is close enough to what most of you think. We know.

If you go inside the mind of one who is confined and unable to go outside, you find that they are somewhat cramped and feel that others are doing better or worse than they are. We want you to sit within the mind today and admit that you are confined too much to be able to say you are Maya. You are. Say it!

You will find that the idea of being an indigenous person living off the Earth is much admired, but even they do not want to live that way. Why? The Earth has progressed and left without delay much of the archaic ways in order to save itself from unrest. If you have nothing to eat or have no bed to sleep in that is not wet, you will want to do more and more to upset everyone who does have more. Think that over now.

If you were a Maya of the old way, and the leaders took away all that you worked for all day, what do you think you would want to do? War!

If those leaders were wary and agile in every way, they would claim you were betrayed by enemies who lived far away so you could turn your spleen upon them and not look at the leadership that is taking what you prepare for your kin. It worked then and it continues to work now in spots on Earth that are still not pure, but what do you want the Maya to speak of about then?

We changed the course of the last sentence and went into the next bend. Could you follow us or was your mind so set on one idea that it could not go into the other? Again, look at yourself and see who is in now. Are you able to say to you now and then that you are conceited? Are you able to say you smile yet do not feel it within? Are you able to lie to you all the while you lie to others? Look at you now.

When you are able to uncover a sin within, what do you do with it? What do you want from the one next to you or sitting beside you? Are you sitting on a bus or in traffic much? What kind of people travel beside you? You and they are the same that day--all trying to move the same way and clogged or flying. What do you want from others? Are you expecting them to work and then turn about and give it all up for you today? You are a bad model of what was thrown away by the Maya in the old days. You will not work long this way.

You must see that idlers have degrees and sit and do nothing for a living only if that is what their home proved to be. If they were raised to be honest and hard working in every way, they work hard today. You see now? You are whoever you were at home before you took off on your own.

If you sit inside a home that you have no part in running today, you are not at home but imprisoned in some way. A hotel is not a home, but you can devote yourself to it and feel right at home if you are at home within it.

Think it over!
What did it prove?

You have two ways to look at you and the home you choose to live in, too, but you are one way or the other today. Look around your home and say, "I am at home." What did you hear right then?

If you cannot hear what is inside you, what would convince you that you cannot work in any way on others, too? You. You alone are able to convince you of what you need to do.

You will find that if you are unhappy today and never do much in really obvious ways in your home, it will stand for a time and then disappear. No house or property will last if not prevented by maintenance to conceal its age and move from one person to another over time.

Your body is aging all the time, but maintaining it with the proper nutrition and stuffing it with enough bulk to make it feel sated enough to live well within you is okay. It keeps you as is. But if you wish to live, you have to maintain the spirit now. You cannot keep the body, regardless of what you may say. The body is on loan today and will spoil or rot or degenerate over time until it hits the spine and you die. You are the spinal fluid, and the column within you channels to others what you do.

You channel?
You do!

What to do today? You have only this moment. Memorize that line and proceed to work on you within you and do whatever the body requires of you first, then go out and see who is about and smile at all who come to see you.

What else is there to do? You will then decide each moment what is good for you to do. If you put off living today, you will not continue to live. If you decide to live for another today, it will stop and you will resent that you gave this day to someone who is not with you. Be you and exist within and go outside and prepare to move up to the next plane in a moment or so.

Why else appear on Earth? You want to sow seeds again and grow. When you know why you go and why you sit and what makes you know, you can go. We admit that most of The Maya never fit into the prophetic pictures that many are projecting upon you, but if you do see them inside that work in time, grow and fit. We want you to know what to do with it, so you will know.

Look at you. What do you know? Now you fit in with The Maya and know what you know, or you are unable to do it. Why bother if it is not easy for you to do it? How will you know if you never do it? Why would you grow and be given more to know if you never did this within you? Who are you going to harm if you just sit and merely state that whatever you do within you is being you? You.

Think of all the accomplishments you delay today

What did you see? Are you able to see the sky and realize why it is so high and far away? Are you able to know who else is in the sky and flying above you? No, but you know there are astronauts and airplanes enough to make the Earth seem to be covered at times with human beings hanging in time. But are they up there? Why not lie? Why not say no one exists whom you cannot see every day? You know why. You know, and you see, and you can either agree or disagree, but it will all occur the way that God decrees it anyway.

We see that makes you nervous inside. Why? The ego is sure that you do make a difference today. Why does the mind disappear and then you disagree with the result of your own mind? You do believe? Good! Do the good work you have decided to do within the mind. We will never upset that time, but if you do decide to work in the line of The Maya before you die, please be sure to answer the additional work you have inside.

When you die and survive in the next life, what is this one for? Are you now aware of time? Are you now able to manipulate it? Are you able to sit within it and do nothing that is not good for you and others, too? Are you feeling proud about what you do with you? Do it more.

You are reaching a plateau within you if you are unable to see what others believe. If you love what you do but suspect that others are not as good as you, you will be stopped and unable to grow beyond what you do. Do more to prevent the pride within you ending what you do.

Pride? Yes, pride is the price you pay when you start saying you are better than others in some way. You end your striving then. You stop surviving and begin dying.

You can end your day?
You do it all the time

You are who decides to thrive, then stores it away and does not try to accumulate more. Nevertheless, you are who you are today based on what you decided yesterday. Why say more?

We see the time is now five o'clock in your mind. Do you feel you did a long day's work because you started work at four or did you labor since nine? What time is it in your mind? Three or more is fine, but if you still feel you are at noon or before, you have not worked enough to take time off and sit inside more.

We want you all to sit and work until the decay is scoured away. Why? You are entitled to beam and shine until the end of time.

Be you! Live until you are told to go to the next plane. Should you be aware that in the stars there are those who

Ruth Lee, Scribe

came to Earth to beam others up another day and will arrive here and take you with them somewhere? Why not? It helps you dream.

Respectfully submitted,
Ruth Lee, Scribe
August 23, 1997

Chapter Fifteen

MAYA WORK - FOOD FOR YOU

Nowhere in the Bible of all the Christians we ever knew are there any words to say that you need to eat every day enough food to bring your body out of its stay in idleness or the onset of decay, but there are many lines devoted to what you may not eat in any way. Why? There is nothing in the world today that is not okay, but in those days there were so many illnesses caused by such things as bad meat--most especially pork, that all were advised not to eat such meat and could turn up sick in other ways, too, but today we will say this:

You can eat meat!

What? You thought that meditation would decrease if you ate meat? Why would God produce a source of food for man, then not let you use it for your own best good? You know that blood is able to rebuild better using the blood of another, so why would the blood of healthy animals not help you?

You may point out that pork and other meats are not good today because they are too likely to be fat. Who else is wrong about what the body needs and what you perceive to be the best way to eat for health today? Every body on Earth is being told to not eat and gain weight. As a result, all of you eat too much of whatever you are told is not good for you to eat. We see you are told that sweets are not good to eat, so all of you wallow in sweets. What about tooth decay? No one cares about it, but that is why sweets are obviously not good for you. If you wash clean the mouth once you eat sweets, what else will go wrong? All of you have consumed food and then burped. You know that you are eating the wrong combination then.

What do you need to accommodate you and the work you do? You need to be able to eat whatever your body requires, so most of you are not able to give up meat completely. If you are, you must assiduously try to find a protein supply that will help you do whatever you are attempting to accomplish at this time. If you do not, your bones and eyes and other elements of the body cannot thrive.

Be good to your Earthly home!

What kind of man or woman tells a child to eat all they want? The kind who is prone to let them do whatever they want. If you cannot control the food a child consumes, you have yielded to the foolish appetites of those too young to be able to yet know what they need to live to be a success. You are failing them if that is what you do now. You cannot expect a child to get good grades and pass all tests if you never try to see what they need. Try to find out over time what is best for their individual needs.

How can you prescribe a food that is best for you to eat and work with over time? Try a test. Look at what you eat today and see if you can eat less, or increase the vitamins and minerals you need. If you cannot find the best way to begin right now to take stock of the way you eat, when do you think you will do it? When you are ill! If you are ill and have no clue about what you do, you normally return in a haze to doing whatever you usually do until the illness repeats and comes back to you.

When a friend is sick and even you notice that they look terrible, do you say that they must have eaten something that did not help them in any way? No, you blame helpers or the doctors of suffering people and excuse the patients of abusing their body--until you discover that the same thing does not happen to you or others, too.

You in time will align with all people who are on Earth to work on the Earth, but you all need to preserve the Earth fully and become more dedicated to working for it than you are now. Why not try to make nutrition a prime cause for all people on Earth now? It would help you and others to work in the proper love of the life you all have within you. This would then prevent some peoples from growing stronger than others or tormenting those who are suffering the most from failing to be able to end this life when it is through.

What? You think that proper nutrition will end the life of this you? What? You do! If you were sure that what you now eat was bad for you, and most of you eventually say that at some point in each day, why do you continue to eat what will end your work here? You do not believe you personally need to work on building energy within you. You believe that you are perfect, and if that impression is jostled for a moment, you run to the doctor. What is worse? Not caring about you or trusting another to put you back together when you have no interest in taking care of you. Decide and move forward.

If you cannot decide what to do, then do what seems to be the most realistic way to stray out of the pattern you live today. If your mind is so closed to new ideas that you cannot do anything new, you die inside the mind and you cannot find anyone who will help you.

Why not climb the stairs one at a time?

If you find your temple is in your mind, be there! If stairs are not in your temple, where do you place them? We would climb stairs all the time, but you never dare. You prefer to say steps are not good for you or will endanger you, but that is not true if you take care of you.

When the heart declines to accept any more of the stress you and your mind provide all the time, *it* will decide to quit and not sit. If you cannot stop your arteries from widening and cutting into the supply of blood all the time, when do you intend to stop it and do what you need to do to exist?

What ideas come to you when we talk about the body, health, your role in playing and practicing wisdom within you in a medical way? Do you feel that you cannot possibly know enough today to take care of you in any real way? What to do when the mind says what you need to do is impossible?

'We want all of the people on Earth to stand in a line and talk constantly at one time.' What if that message was beamed to you? Would you do it? No, but most of you stand around now and talk to no one about what you are. Why? You fear that you may die and no one will understand why you came to Earth. We do.

The Word of The Maya

When you arrive on Earth and have a decent reception and a crew gathered around you who welcome you, you thrive. It is otherwise only if the body God prepared was not as *good* as it was when it was first delivered inside. The body normally rejects a *bad* birth, but today all of you fool around inside all the time to stop the process of what you call sex and what you want now. Then you say that you have trouble in other ways.

You all have trouble with sex, if that is what you try to stop in some way. If the mind cannot accept that sex is a way to stimulate you to make more of you, then you have truly strayed from the way. But if you think only of procreation and what it means to you and those around you, will you enjoy sex as much as others say? You all talk too much about sex today!

When you do, you do. If you talk, you never do. What is so much an effort that it makes you all work on a subject that others 'just know'? You are upset inside over a number of other issues you do not wish to continue.

You are going to upset the delicate tissue if you do not flush the body much. What if you only rinsed the dishes of stuff and never used anything to clean them thoroughly at least once a day? You would be sick in a month--if not sooner for some. Why? You have microbes on the hands and in the mouth that help you touch and feel and swiftly reveal if food is not good to chew, but most of you do not clean your mouth enough. You chew rotten food? You do.

If you chop up a cow, then sear it in a flash or two, are you eating the cow? You are not trying to eat a cow, but if you wanted the cow to be new and not able to taste good to you, maybe you would eat only fresh meat. Most of you never do. You eat what is sold to you.

We would produce a calf that is not fatted, but you do not approve of that. We would not let the sow get so upset that her crew is taken from her, but you do. Why not let them all know that you need them to work for you? Are you an animal to work with and do work for you? You are if you never star in your own life now.

If you spar with others constantly--thrilled to win a game or two, you need much fuel. You burn calories foolishly this way. You do not need to be given more energy to fight again that day, because you burn out internally and the mind gives up after awhile. That is why you must rest and eat properly.

If you sit down and the work you produce then is not good for you, what do you say about it? If you sit down and the work you do inside you is good, but the mind does not say that it is, what do you do with it?

Work out the spleen on what you mean. If the liver is what generates a new body for you, what do you give it to make it live better and do more for you? Alcoholic beverages stimulate the liver until it overworks reproducing you. Are you kicking the habit or not able to abolish what is poisoning you?

**Look at you!
You are who does it to you.**

We never do a thing to you or your mind or whatever, but some of you have already begun to say we are able to help you unwind. Who knows that? Your mind decides.

The Word of The Maya

If you sit in a parlor with others who are dining around you, are you going to expect them to pay for you? You do. You expect that if you pay for a meal or two that others will deal fairly with you, but some never do. Eat only what you can see being prepared in front of you if you are sure others are not going to cook like you do.

What can you make of such a statement coming from The Maya about what you do daily? You cannot imagine anyone ever preparing a meal only for you, but you do. Why do you let others determine what is good for you and treat it as though it were what they wanted to give away and not eat that day? You are not able to see what we mean? You are trying to ignore that the body is tissue, which you need to live like this, thus must never ignore.

Eat what you have grown and what grows nearest to your home. If that is not good or there is not enough, prepare to save your own work more by eating at home and cooking what you know is fresh and will help you make a delicious dish.

You think of art when you see The Maya? You are the art of you in all the things you do, but eating is the only art most of you enjoy every day. Why? All of you, all over the Earth, are complaining about water. You do not always drink the water of your own land and what is close by. If you want the minerals that are dissolved in the water around your home, you should drink that water first! Does that sound like sound advice to anyone now? You must be very thirsty or worried to buy bottled water that is created far from your home--or have money to burn.

You hate to burn? You water too many lawns and gardens now, but none of you is alarmed. If the house goes down in flames, you attack anyone who is not there immediately to do what you should be prepared to do yourself--put it out and get it back in shape as soon as you can for your sake. If you expect 'the public' to always take care of you, you will find out too late you made a huge mistake.

The Scribe lives with a tribe of vigilantes who always try to buy books today, but she is not that way. Why? She is tired of doing what others prescribe and even wonders why you will want to buy a book about The Maya who are not in this place or time, but she intuitively knows inside that you need the message from us at this time. What does this say about the mind? The mind would not let the Scribe write a line if Spirit was not able to more than adequately make the day come through time as the Scribe wants to live now. Think over that line.

If you think that others owe you a living or that they should scribe or write up your life and you do nothing with it, you will not survive beyond the time you live now. If you think others will have to do more and more for you, not caring about what they have to do for you, you are not sane. Get into the life you are and serve you! How do you service you when you have not done what the body wants? You first seek to see what is wrong.

Look inside you

First, imagine that you can see the bowel. Look at it and what it contains and clean out any remains. Let it flow as if down a drain.

If you cannot do that at all, you are dying from the food inside you. You have to be clean! If you are not clean, you sometimes die right away, but mostly you cannot be you or stay lean.

What to do if you never care about you?

If so, you have now arrived at the end of the line. You are not able to do whatever you want and will continue to deal poorly with you and not care what happens inside. You will let your insides rot.

What if the mind says you can live all the time? You will not take care to see that you live at least today without pain. The mind will take over and desert you at the end. The mind is not the friend you think of when you are on the mend, but it is what made it happen again. Your mind cannot desert you? It leaves you all the time when you are not in your own state of mind.

As you sleep, where does the mind sit? If you sleep and dream, what does the mind think? Are you able to cognitively open the mind and find the dreams within you all the time? You are not able to understand, so stop wasting your mind and the time you have left to work on time.

If all you do, and the amazing things you could be, were to all blend into something concrete, what would you do?

Think over that line

What did you do? Are you sure that you have enough left inside you to do all that you hope to be and do for You? Look at the body now. Are you convinced that it is capable of paying for you to move up in rank again?

Ruth Lee, Scribe

Look again at the body and what the mind is trying to say all the time. What does your mind say about you now? Write up a line or two to introduce you to the idea that you create this being and never mind it, or you are creatively being you. Write down what you eventually want to be.

_____
_____
_____
_____
_____
_____
_____
_____

Need more room? You cannot see how much energy it takes to write, let alone believe, and then to finally achieve, but write now and see.

_____
_____
_____
_____
_____

What was your mind achieving when you wrote each line? Write what you see now.

_____
_____
_____
_____
_____
_____

Are you now able to visualize the crowds of others who are about to survive and climb into the sky with you? Look at them and achieve a more realistic image of that time.

What did you see?

Are you incapable of visualizing within you today what you will be or see in another day? You are then not using the soul's way to survive. If you could, you would be clairvoyant today and able to perceive the easiest way to achieve all that you believe. If you do that now, congratulate you on being able to ignore all the many who do not see it as living proof that God does prepare you.

You must shut off the mind to meditate? You do it anyway, but now you will control the mind more than you did before. If you tell the mind to meditate at will, does it work well? Are you prepared to sit? Are you breathing without obstruction now and able to feel you have eaten enough? If not, you do not feel well. If you are tired, you will sleep instead of telling the body to meditate and go within you. The body must be helped if it is that tired now.

You are told by hints and whispers whenever the body is unwell, but you shout over it. What? You heard the word. If you cannot think of you or what you do and what others are constantly trying to teach you to do for you, you are not able to remember the world. Either you have never been on Earth before this experiment within you, or you are totally ignorant of Earth and what it did before to each of you here now.

Most people today lived on Earth when it was difficult to avoid war and famine and all sorts of physical decay, so you

Ruth Lee, Scribe

are unhappy if anyone around who is younger than you dies. Why? You want to survive longer today than you did when you worked on Earth before.

If you find the lines are too silly at times to submit them to your mind, you are trying to say you honestly know more than 'they'. Who are 'they'? This is always someone unlike you.

If you want to someday die and submit to the trial of being judged for not being you, pray to leave while the list is shorter than it will be if you continue to be so conceited now. You will comment please.

Write down all the things that please you most about your life today.

_____
_____
_____
_____
_____
_____
_____
_____
_____
_____
_____
_____
_____

We cannot fit all of you on a page? You cannot, if you have to write lines and lines over and over and not see that you repeat you all day.

The Word of The Maya

When the lines come to you, and you see that you are not working hard enough to do all the things you know you want to do, what comes next? You reduce your view of YOU, or yell, or compare you to others who do it. Yes, that is what envy and jealousy do to you. They help you diminish you.

When you say someone else is better than you, and you do that when you are jealous of him or her, you find that no one else is as interested in you then. Why not just be you and be content to fly to the top of your own mind? The sick mind will not let you.

If your mind is sick over the amount of work you must do, who will know what to do? You. The higher You knows what to do; and if that is a problem for you, then the highest being you are now will overcome the incessant beating of your own drum. You will be told what to do? You are being told, but might not want to know what to do.

What makes you pray all day, then not live that way? You. The work you do in this world is not what will help you on the final day. But if you do not live every single day for you, you will have no life to look forward to because you will have to return and do this one over again for You.

What about that paragraph made you laugh? You are upset more than you are happy about what you read? You are then filled with dread.

What makes a soul depart this life and dread to be read a lesson about the life they chose to do? YOU. The many things you tell others bring a burden to the mind. You have to pursue all these things for you then. Do not ask for work or brag about what you do unless you do want to work on you. The work will spring up fast if you do. You may not be able to pursue half of what you ask for today, but ask to at least delay the onslaught of more work that can upset your departure for a single day.

We are all here!

The line that makes all of you combine is not here in the work of The Scribe, but in the mind of all who are on time. You all are reading more and more and doing less if you cannot combine the lessons of more than one scribe and see what is there between all the lines.

You have to go back and reread those lines if you cannot repeat the meaning and feel complete.

If you are done with a life, and asked to refer for a moment of time to what you did while on Earth, what do you think you do now that is going to be true then?

What did you do? Are you able to now see that you are who does not believe or believes that you can achieve all that you do believe? What is coming to you? If you are able to sit in the middle of a reading and visualize a line, please do it now.

What did you do? Are you still trying to read as fast as those around you? What do you feel will happen to you if they beat you in speed? What will happen if you never read? What are you reading if you speed through each page without perceiving? You cannot fool you now.

You are now aware that deep within you, you now have to square up and do what you came to do. It is there and working on you.

The Word of The Maya

What did you do?
Are you able to balance you?

If you feel topsy-turvy or upside down, please enter You now and find out what to do. If you cannot find time to align the spine, then you are too upset to be you. The body requires that you take time to be you. Do you even care now about what you do to the body and what it is preparing for you? You are now if you read and rehearsed all the words. You are in deep despair inside the body now if you heard and did nothing to reverse that despair over what you are doing to you. If you believe that the body produces you, you are right to assume that the mood is prepared mainly in the artery line and helps you to move. If you believe all moods come into you, you are crude and will not move and do what you need--work on you.

If the mood of day and night cannot coincide, you will feel that you do not do what you want to do; but if you are able to do whatever you want and do not, you disappoint you to the point of depressing you. Why not let the work you do help you? The next session will help or depress you, but do this lesson now.

You have to change you if you expect to be Maya and go beyond this group of beings who are waiting to stand beside you. Who are The Maya? You are one and have decided to work beside the others who are gathering now to stand beside you.

What? You can deliberately try to make up a story that will not combine over time with what you have within you, but The Maya will not be there if you do that. You are able to assume safely that you control the mind? You never do if you cannot do what you are prepared to do--be you.

Ruth Lee, Scribe

Act today and see what happens to you!

When you are you and able to stand up and do, are you doing it? What do you think of people who are not like you? Work on that view, too, since you came to Earth to learn to respect all aspects of You. If you cannot, you will return to do it over--at least once in that role, so do it right now. Change your perception of whoever is hurting you to know you better than you do now.

Some of the work you do will help you, but what if the work you do is never for you? You will end up with a lot of work to do yet. You will not be able to ascend in the end. You will lose a lot of the friends you worked with now and tried to help get beyond Earth. Some of you think that you have to do that or you will never be able to ascend. What a way to see you! You have to mend.

You must see that God created and made you to be you because you are worth it and will be able to do it and ascend in the end. Does anything about that sentence disturb you within? You are then in trouble from within and have to ascend or not, yet you have not been able to live for you.

We want you to ascend? Who is in the work if not everyone? Who on Earth is not of The Maya inside in some way today? You, if you cannot blend or bend into the work of the stage of development where we are now.

We all are here to ascend! Are you?

Respectfully submitted,
Ruth Lee, Scribe
August 25, 1997

The Word of The Maya

Chapter Sixteen

MAYA MYSTERIES WITHIN THE VEIL

Do you see within the veil and what it means? Are you able to see what seems to mean one thing to you and something totally different to others, and still not know the difference? What does it mean?

The veil is a shroud that clings to the way people see the Earth and what it appears to be, but within the seams of each belief system is a word or two that seems to bring a release of all that was stated before in this time. What does that mean? There are things you cannot know in this dream of a life on Earth, but when it is over you will see that the seams opened and closed whenever you were close to the mysteries of your own life, birth, death, and other remote possibilities, but never when you were close to who you are and why you are and what you are.

You will not boast!

Is that the same thing, as you will not talk about you? No, but some of you know that talking about you makes the ego grow and you feel that it can hurt you. Others reveal much about you, but nobody knows you. If you talk about you and the work you do, it is then a way of admiring or hating you in the same way, so only the vain and the damaged egos do boast too much.

If your ego is damaged, what can you do to remain on Earth without undoing the work you want to do? You can learn to stop and listen to others and not be tempted to talk without permission. You can and will do whatever is still within your heart and not there by any admission on your part, because that is the channel within you that cannot be opened or closed without heart.

You can still be happy and ecstatic that you did something you never thought you could do, and did it for you and others are happy you did it, but do not ask them to talk about it, too. Just enjoy you. Enjoy those who are also growing with you. Live for the moment! Do what you ought. If you do these things and they succeed, no one has to hear a word from you. You will be unique and quite beyond the belief of the present moment.

If the present time is unkind, what makes you mind time so much of the time? You all are not doing what you came to be in many instances of this place and time because you are beyond relief. You are too tired. You are so tired you cannot think and orderly proceed to do whatever you believe.

If the artist is tired and beyond relief, the art does not end, but most of the output is old and tired. You are not able to function well if you never sleep, so get on with it. Sleep produces dreams and dreams are the veil beyond these seams. Dream!

If you never enter the dream or the seam of life you have inside, you cannot open and see the why and the when of this time, but it will still be. It has to be. It is time, and it is inside the mind all the time you are alive this time. Why? Go inside and see.

Did you go without hesitation into your own third eye? Fine. Did you mind receiving a command to work in this way? Then you will find in time you are not humble enough to arrive in a line and stand waiting until all are ready to be denied or accepted at one time. You are not alive, merely doing whatever someone else says not to do, and daring not to be you. Be wise!

Listen with your eyes

What can you see if the eyes are blinded by something you had no control over and blindness lasted into this time? You will see many things the sighted cannot believe, but none now want to tell those who do *see* what is in the world. Why? They are afraid of it. Afraid they will be shouted at, but it is there within for them to see now.

What arrives when you cast your eyes inside? What if a devil or angel seemed to arrive? What does it mean? Write down now what you have seen, and why it is there, and how much you can see of it, and why it is not going to harm you at all.

If you cannot do this, you have had a long line of descent into this world that will not permit you to ascend at the end. You must do it! Trust us on this.

If you refuse to practice your art, you admit that you are not willing to work for anything that you came to do for You. If you are tired of being here within You, imagine for a bit what You could do with you if you were more willing to be you now. If you cannot do it, you are surprised that others do it all the time. Admit it!

If you cannot admit that others are smarter or wiser and more able to get on in the world than you are, how can you admit that you are losing it to others in spiritual work? You do that all the time when you say over and over and louder and louder that you do not dream and you do not think dreams mean anything to anyone else.

If your mind refuses to let you dream, that is one thing, but if the mind is drugged or unable to listen for a long time to the messages of Spirit and goes into the next world without any of them getting to you, what does that mean? You did it to you!

Figure out why you decided not to live and wanted to separate from Spirit. Once you do that, sit and write down why you are willing to live on Earth but never visit the next work. If you can write it out and pass it around, others might even listen and want to do it, too, but probably only those who love you will permit you to do it.

When you write a poem and it is good, and you got a lot out of it, is it time to publish your work and demand a dime for it? Not if it is your limit. However, if you are given a limitless quantity of poetry all the time and have nothing you can do with it, it is time to publish the work. Time will be there to do it, but will you be able to get a dime for doing it? You must not forget the lesson of The Scribe and how it took a tribe to do it. If you think you can do it, try to follow her way to the top by working through others and find someone who will listen. There will not be many who are enough like you to buy, but all you need is one. If you sell one person your work, you can boast that you are the author of whatever, but does it work? You will find out in time.

What to do with the author in you when you want to write and no one is by your side to read it? You preach it then? No, but you can teach it to others. The Scribe wrote a book many years before this one about the way a woman works today, then preceded to work and live that same way. Today she is the woman she wrote about then but never realized until she scribed these lines. She has a polished edge. She is a scribe and cries as she sees these lines. You see, she had to fulfill that dream before she could beam out to others on Earth that she deserves to be heard and her work deserves to be seen. There are many scribes and others alive who are working on Earth also, but all are working at work they like on the inside.

It is time for all of you to follow a tribal line and form an avenue of time. If you can follow your dream to the end of the time in which you are now alive and do all that you dream, will it all prevail? It is the veil. The dream is a mind, a body, a time, a national line, and an inspiration to do more for everybody in the time you are there. If you cannot see the veil, dream and see what is keeping you there.

If your veil is not open to the world out there, you see only the small group of *you* on Earth, but it is a huge beam that makes you all seem so close. You are Earth! You are not a small planet that makes tons of garbage from what is pristine, but a group who are trying to boast to the planets above you that you know the most. You are totally ignorant of us.

We know you, but you refuse to trust us. What do you do when you do not trust others? You do not trust you.

If your mind is open to us, The Maya, you cannot know mistrust. If you are able to sense devotion and duty among us to the work of those stranded in time and on Earth, you cannot know why you boast or why you must help others. You are not able to ascend or move around the bend. The bend is ahead, but can you move you to go beyond it and see what is there and will be?

If you can bend time into another line, will you? You do it all the time. You are all of you in a line and able to bend it all the time, but time is not an issue any longer for those who are able to stand up and be strong. You are to do what you want, but God of All calls those who listen to do more and more and stand taller than ever before.

The Word of The Maya

What time is it? You know, but refuse to grow if you cannot see why it is the issue of this time on Earth for those now about to descend until the end. You may wonder why all the people on Earth fear the time when a century unwinds and grow more spiritual then, but it is a cycle that is inside the mind of those who care about time. If you never cared about time, what would end at 2000 or whenever? If you never counted on a hand or foot what you do or know, how would you know the time? You would circle the globe and explore what others do to count and time the Earth and find out what it does in order to be productive for you, too. You would know a lot more than you do now about why time is and does not exist--except in the minds of people like you.

You know? You do, but most of you have to return to school to be reminded to look inside you. Today no one removes the shroud of ignorance from you unless you do. Teachers never seek the oldest or wisest or do more and more with those who seek to learn whatever, but spend time on the ones who cannot do anything without them. Why? It is a type of job security within an unkind world that makes you want to cling to those who need you most and ignore those who are glorious.

If you are unable to sing about the talents of the young, find out what makes the old smug and want to run the young out of town if not vanity in accomplishments that no longer exist. The old are supposed to take care of the young. If you are over 21, you are responsible for every young person who is near or with you anywhere. It is the way, always, but today many need to repeat that lesson of Earth the hard way. If you refuse, you will be blamed for contributing to the delinquency of a minor only by the current law? You are doing your own soul greater harm than if you were to commit the murder of another adult. You are not to ever harm a child!

Ruth Lee, Scribe

If your mind is revolted by the death of someone, or you stay out of all arguments today in order not to be alarmed in any way, are you pious, devoted, or just not willing to work to solve the problems of today? What makes you so vain that you cannot do anything to solve another's problem who is in so deep that they cannot speak or perhaps even sleep?

We notice you are all totally beyond recall when it comes to remembering the seven to nine dreams you have any time you sleep deep enough to dream. What does this mean? You cannot go within the seams of most dreams and find the meaning of the mystery.

If the mystery of life is revealed in dreams, what does it mean when you ignore all that dreams seem to mean? It is a way of saying 'I am okay, but it doesn't help me to study dreams.' Why not try to use all the gifts you have inside and accept no abuse?

If you are vain and others say you are not as good as they are, do you run them down or do you enter their work and try to do it better than they do it? We want the latter personality to step up at this time and try to undo the work of The Scribe. If you can sit at a computer and type up a sheet or two in an hour, with so much you do not know coming out of you, you can scribe, too. But if you are unable to type a chapter or two in an hour and do it perfect enough that others do not need to proofread it, but you do, then you are a Scribe as great at this time as Ruth Lee. We want you to move into the same line.

If you are sitting at a computer and reading at the same time, what do you see in front of you if not a screen writing what you do? Can you see that line was garbled because you cannot do two things well at the same time.

If your work is so garbled at times that you lie about you at home or to others trying to make them believe you achieve more than you do, you deceive them and ruin your mind. You cannot lie to you! If you do, you will be reminded over and over again that you have to do whatever you said, until it stops reminding you and accepts that you are a liar in time regardless of what you do now.

When you meet a liar on the street and never check to see that their lie was meant to cover a degree of 'inconfidence' within that man or woman then, will you realign your map or your plan because they told you the wrong address or directions again? You might believe them, but only for a few more times. The mind is exactly like that. If you constantly lie, the mind does not listen to you. If you lie now and then, you are constantly reminded that you lied about whatever. So if you lie all the time, you will believe that all things taught you about others is untrue. For this reason and others, we want no liars to now join the work we do. Do you?

If you work in a line and it is time to ascend or develop again, do you want the line to stand in place or move more and more toward the next place? You move. You all do. You all are moving now as never before, but most do not know what to do and why.

What do you move for?

If your mind constantly has no good times, are you responsible for that? You are, and you know you are, but you will constantly blame others around you. You will in time criticize others who have a great life or enjoy having a good time, but usually you will lie. You will tell others you are having a great life, but The Scribe and others are able to see beyond it at this time. In time, all of you will split the veil in two and be able to walk behind it. Go now and prepare for that day and see what you will wear.

Why wear anything at that time? You want to know? You always consider the garment of others before you admit them into your presence to boast that you know who they are, so why would you suddenly not care what you wear when the final moments of Earth are here? You see? You do not question your own motives enough.

If you can discern the meaning of a person in a moment, what does that mean? If you can discern the meaning of a being not on Earth at this moment, what does that mean and why do you know it? Are you able to progress into more difficult lessons on Earth now? If you can easily answer all there is to know about these three questions, you are ready to ascend. If not, please remain enclosed in your own Earth for a moment and study wherever you are not able to boast. We need you the most.

If you can do the work and carry the torch that lights the path for the universe to provide you all with lives you want at the last, will that path be wide enough for all those whom you love? Are you even talking to them about it or do you admit to anyone that you are reading this book?

What is it that makes you nervous and unhappy to speak to someone about what you do when alone? Think on it. If your mind is in reverse or refuses to accept that there is a better way to live, you will live over and over the same situation until the end of your days. We want you to join The Maya, too, but only you can do it. You will now go and accept the final lessons, or you will not, but not because you were not taught to respect what you do for YOU.

The Word of The Maya

You are now dismissed from the critical issues of this book about You and The Maya within you, but do you see that it can be used by others who are not like you, too? If you cannot, you merely boast. If you do, teach it to others and respect what they will teach you, too. We need you, but first continue with the work that we did for you and asked you to do before we ended that work and became one with you.

Did that last sentence insert any more energy in you? If so, you did that to you.

Go now and finish the work you came to do. Forget that you are a Maya, too, but do not admit that to anyone who has work to do. You will not be liked by others if you do? Who cares about you? Only you are able to despise you, so don't do it!

We are about to end this lesson on you and time and why the Maya are here within You? You will or you won't continue. We do need time to sit inside and visit with you, but will you provide it? That is the real issue of you now.

Work now to provide a space within the day for you to sit and not criticize you. We will then be glad to sit with you and do whatever you need to do to inspire you.

Work today to build a better relationship with YOU and everything will be better in the days remaining for whatever you do. You either start now or you never do.

End Notes

When a project of this magnitude is created and maintained and delivered in a day or two, many think that it does not take pain and energy and much explanation to get the thought across, but it does. Today, we wish to help you understand what The Maya do with work that must go through the veil and into time in the hope that it will help you do the same with your mind.

The mind is not easy on you or on anything that comes through to you from others, so it is hard to get it to relax and sit back and just let your spirit do the work. It often refuses to meditate, or just relax, because it is ever on guard and vigilant that you might want to change you. Once a habit it is established, it is difficult to remove or to exclude, but you can do it.

Meditate or sit silently and try to clear your mind as often during each day as you can. Once you master this, you can master anything you must do or have to do to ascend and leave this world behind to those who will undertake its lessons and plans. You do not have to repeat this lesson again. If you have no clue about how to ascend again, then we are providing you with material you can use to decide when and where and if you want to do it now or come back again and live through all of this.

Nothing weird, nothing strange, just plain words about a subject that is too deep to explain. You must feel it. The Spirit of YOU and You and you will carry you through.

We have no worries that you will not be able to do the work, but you may have to hurry if your mind is not able to stop worrying a lot. Take care of you and what you do and the world will be able to help you ascend, too, once again. This is truth. You have to get used to it if you never speak it yourself or see it in your career or within your sphere. Once you get it, you will find your way home.

Respectfully submitted,
Ruth Lee, Scribe
May 21, 2004
11 Ben, 0 Pax

About the Author

To introduce you to Ruth Lee, Scribe, you must grasp that her work differs from traditional Scribes in that she picks up intuitively what is constantly being channeled, from sources beyond this world to each of us. She can instantaneously sort through millions of incoming signals and their links in order to transcribe such wisdom for our daily use.

When scribing what comes through her Divine source, Ruth Lee enters an altered state of mind. As she writes rapidly, she simultaneously reads the text aloud--almost as fast as others talk, but she has no memory of the work when done.

That is just about all you can know about this Spiritual Scribe...the rest is mystery.

Printed in the United States
27201LVS00003B/316-339